Rave Revues

A cookbook
with the best recipes
from 240 kitchens
to benefit the
Lakewood Center for the Arts

LAKEWOOD
CENTER
ASSOCIATES
LAKE OSWEGO, OREGON

ACKNOWLEDGEMENTS

We wish to thank the following for their time, advice, and technical assistance; they have truly been our "angels":

Roger C. Abele, Paul Amlin, Bruce Craig, Janet Graves, Michael Hopkins, Kraig W. Kramers, the Lake Oswego School District, Don New, Richard Pearson, and Gayland Rogers.

Designed by • Graphic Media, Inc
Typeset by • Paul O. Giesey/Adcrafters
Printed by • RR Donnelley Norwest, Inc. / WCP Division
Bindery by • Lincoln & Allen

Printed in the United States of America

International Standard Book Number 0-9617239-0-4
Library of Congress Catalogue Card Number 86-82326
Copyright © 1986 by Lakewood Center Associates
P.O. Box 274 • Lake Oswego, Oregon 97034

First Printing: October 1986
Second Printing: August 1988
Third Printing: June 1994

Additional copies may be purchased from Lakewood Center Associates at the above address.

PROLOGUE

Lakewood Center is for all the arts—visual and performing. The Lake Oswego Community Theater with its 200 seats is the central focus, with art galleries and music and dance studios radiating from it. A pre-school which emphasizes the arts is rewarding to those members of the community who remember Lakewood as a school, the first in Oswego. Lakewood Center benefits all age groups and is for all the public to enjoy.

Lakewood Center Associates was formed as a support group. This cookbook is one of the group's projects, designed to publicize Lakewood Center as well as to raise funds for its purchase and development.

Because the theater is at the heart of Lakewood, a theatrical theme was chosen for this book. President and Mrs. Reagan, well known for their support of the performing arts, have kindly sent us three of their favorite recipes, and many other celebrities related to the theater and to Oregon have sent us theirs (see "celebrity recipes" in index). We gratefully thank these supporters as well as all those friends of Lakewood who contributed recipes to Rave Revues. All recipes may not be original, but they are favorites and were donated to advance the arts through private initiative.

Lake Oswego is a suburb of Portland, Oregon, located in the Pacific Northwest, a land of bounty from the sea and the land. The present widespread interest in food and the art of cooking is prevalent, and perhaps began here with James Beard, America's beloved writer on foods who was an Oregon native.

Over 750 recipes were sent in by the many supporters of the Center. Space determined that 350 recipes would be published. Those recipes sent by celebrities were left untouched, for we felt their words and their entries were like a signature. All recipes were tested at least once and carefully edited for order and consistency.

Those of us involved in Rave Revues now know why many of our own (previously) favorite cookbooks have been those published by community groups. Thousands of hours of work, all volunteer, have been necessary to this production. They have been rewarding hours, and we recommend the experience; we also recommend Rave Revues.

RAVE REVUES PRODUCTION CREW

Director • Judy McCuddy
Assistant Director • Judy Kershaw

*The crew whose work behind the scenes
brought* Rave Revues *to reality.*

Sali Bernhardt
Ailsa Bloodworth
Mary Beth Burpee
Susan Cameron
Marlis Carson
Priscilla Coombs
Maxyne Davis
Ann Deering
Mary Deich
Dee Denton
Stephanie Detjens
Dorothy Drinker
Ann Durfee
Barbara Dutton
Beth Gerber
DeDe Gillespie
Katherine Jefferson
Charlotte Kern
Ann McGranahan
Kathy Lindemann
Laura Mold
Janet Moore
Virginia Mullen
Ann North
Sally Robinson
Elizabeth Ross
Dorie Russell
Sally Stark
Carol Strader
Marianne Swinford
Susan Reinhart
Gerri Tisdel
Nancy Todd
Adrienne Tromley
Marjorie Warne
Dorothy Westlund
Jean Young

PROGRAMME

Script

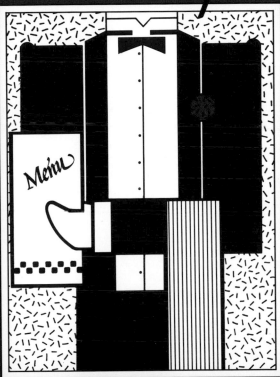

MENUS

---◆---

FROM THE TERRACE

A summer brunch.

*Sunshines

Scrambled Eggs Garnished with Chopped Green Onions

*Chicken Livers Caramel

*Northwest Cinnamon Rolls
or
*Cinnamon Roll-ups

Coffee   Tea

---◆---

THE EGG AND I

A hearty brunch menu.

*Brian's Golden Gin Fizzes

*Pecan Cheese Bites

*Frozen Fruit Compote

*Fancy Egg Scramble

Bacon   Ham   Sausage

*Razudan Muffins

*Maple Crumb Muffins

*Orange Cranberry Bread

*Grapenut Loaf

Coffee   Tea

A CHRISTMAS CAROL
The traditional Christmas luncheon of Oswego Garden Club.

Freshly Toasted and Salted Pecans and Walnuts
Champagne or Gewurztraminer

*Sausage Soufflé

*Crunchy Tomato Aspic

*Savory Bread

*Lemon Snow Pudding with Raspberry Sauce

BAREFOOT IN THE PARK
A picnic.

*Gazpacho

Pita Bread

*Green Pasta Salad

*Chicken Salad Lu Chow

*Miniature Orange Muffins

*Almond Squares

*Shandy Gaffs   Lemonade

SUMMER AND SMOKE
A barbecue.

*Hawaiian Stuffed Lychee Nuts

*Hammer's Superb Barbecued Salmon

*Barley Pilaf

*Roquefort Onions
Chardonnay or Pinot Noir

*Lakeside Frozen Lemon Pie

A LITTLE NIGHT MUSIC

An appetizer buffet.

Cocktails   Wine

*Brie in Puff

*Liverwurst Pâté

A Selection of Cheeses

*Seafood Mousse

*Miniature Quiche Lorraine

*Sayadia Tahini

*Chutney Cream Cheese

*Hatch Road with Crudités Platter

Assorted Crackers and Bread Rounds

*Meltaways

*Pecan Turtle Bars

THE WINTER'S TALE

A souper supper by the fire.

Dry Sherry

Almonds

*Oven Baked Split Pea Soup

*LeTourneau's Salad

*Baked Cheese Fingers

*Mile High Lemon Pie

Cinnamon Tea   Coffee

I REMEMBER MAMA

A dinner of old favorites.

*Brownell's Orange Salad Mold

*Our Favorite Ham

*Swiss Green Beans

*Corn Custard

*Tennessee Tomato Relish

*Gammy's Coffee Can Bread

*Best-in-the-West Berry Cobbler

GREEN PASTURES

An Easter dinner.

*Chilled Zucchini Soup

*Lamb Crown Roast with Carrot Stuffing

Fresh Steamed Asparagus with Lemon Butter
Oregon Pinot Noir or Cabernet Sauvignon

*Watercress Salad

*Lemon Lime Soufflé

DINNER AT EIGHT

An elegant dinner party menu.

*Vichyssoise with Chive Garni
White Cabernet or Pouilly-Fumé

*Cold Asparagus with Prosciutto and Parmesan
with
Hot Crunchy French Bread
Chianti Classico

*Coquilles St. Charles

*Carrots Julienne
1er Cru Chablis or Alsatian Riesling

*Floating Islands with Crème Anglaise

HOME IS THE HUNTER

A game dinner.

*Crab Pâté with Mayonnaise
with
Bread or Crackers
Oregon Riesling

*Venison Steak with Cracked Pepper

*Wild Rice and Mushroom Casserole
Cabernet Sauvignon

*Green Salad with Oregon Blue and Walnuts

*Kirsch Cake

ALL'S WELL THAT ENDS WELL

A dessert buffet.

Champagne

Fresh Fruit Platter

Dessert Cheeses:
Bel Paese and Mascarpone
with
Assorted Crackers

*Capitol Chocolate Torte

*Upside Down Lemon Meringue Pie

*Whiskey Tarts

*Angellica Cookies

*Swedish Nuts

Coffee   Tea

Overture

APPETIZERS

ARTICHOKE APPETIZERS

2 (6-ounce) jars marinated artichoke hearts

1 small onion, finely chopped

2 cloves garlic, minced

4 eggs

¼ cup fine, dry bread crumbs

¼ teaspoon salt

⅛ teaspoon pepper

⅛ teaspoon oregano

⅛ teaspoon Tabasco

8 ounces sharp Cheddar cheese, shredded

⅓ cup Parmesan cheese, grated

2 tablespoons minced parsley

Makes 77 (1-inch) squares.

Drain artichokes; place marinade from 1 jar in skillet. Chop artichokes finely; set aside. Heat marinade over medium heat. Add onion and garlic; sauté until onion is limp but not brown.

In a bowl, beat eggs with a fork. Stir in crumbs and seasonings; add cheeses, parsley, artichokes and onion mixture. Turn into greased 7 x 11-inch baking dish. Bake, uncovered, in 325° oven for about 30 minutes, or until set. Let cool; cut into 1-inch squares. May be served hot or cold.

MUSHROOMS À LA GRECQUE

These travel well; take some along on your next picnic.

1½ pounds small mushrooms

2 cups water

1 cup olive oil

Juice of 1 lemon

1 tablespoon white vinegar

1 stalk celery, sliced

1 clove garlic, mashed

½ teaspoon rosemary

½ teaspoon sage

½ teaspoon thyme

½ bay leaf

¾ teaspoon ground coriander

6 peppercorns

¾ teaspoon salt

Makes about 90.

Combine all ingredients and bring to a boil. Simmer 5 minutes. Pour into a bowl and refrigerate overnight.

Serve with toothpicks or on a bed of lettuce as a first course.

FAR EAST STUFFED MUSHROOMS

Beautiful served in a Chinese soup spoon on a lacquer tray, with kale as a garnish.

1 pound mushrooms, about 1½ inches in diameter

½ pound ground raw pork

¼ cup chopped water chestnuts

¼ cup green onions, minced

1 egg

1 tablespoon soy sauce

1 teaspoon Lawry's seasoned salt

Ground pepper

Melted butter

Sesame seeds, toasted

Makes about 30 to 40.

Remove stems with melon ball cutter; chop half the stems and mix with remaining ingredients.

Roll each mushroom cap in melted butter and fill with meat mixture, using a melon ball cutter and piling high. Generously cover mounds with sesame seeds.

Bake at 350° for 35 minutes. Serve hot as appetizer or as vegetable accompaniment to an entrée. These freeze well.

BACON-STUFFED MUSHROOMS

1 pound medium-sized mushrooms

4 slices bacon, diced

1 medium onion, minced

2 tablespoons green pepper, minced

1 teaspoon salt

⅛ teaspoon pepper

3 ounces cream cheese, room temperature

½ cup bread crumbs, plain or buttered

¼ cup hot water

Makes about 30 to 40.

Clean mushrooms; remove and chop stems. Set aside.

Sauté bacon in skillet. Remove with a slotted spoon and set aside. In bacon fat, sauté onion, green pepper and chopped mushroom stems until tender but not brown; drain. Add salt and pepper.

Soften cream cheese; add bacon and vegetables. Press firmly into mushroom caps, mounding slightly. Place bread crumbs in small bowl. Turn filled mushroom caps upside down in crumbs to coat tops. May be refrigerated or frozen at this point; thaw before baking. Place in 9 x 12-inch baking dish. Add hot water and bake, uncovered, 15 to 20 minutes at 325°.

CURRY SAUCE FOR CRACKERS OR CRUDITÉS

1 hard-cooked egg, finely diced

1 cup mayonnaise

½ teaspoon salt

½ teaspoon ground ginger

¼ teaspoon garlic salt

2 tablespoons green onion, minced

1½ teaspoons curry powder

2 teaspoons lemon juice

Makes 1½ cups.

Combine ingredients in order given. Refrigerate until served. Excellent served with crackers.

CHILI ARTICHOKE DIP

1 (14-ounce) can plain artichoke hearts, drained

1 (4-ounce) can green chiles, chopped

1 cup mayonnaise

1 cup grated Parmesan cheese

Makes 3 cups.

Combine all ingredients in food processor or blender until smooth. Pour into small casserole that can be used for serving.

Bake at 350° for 20 minutes. Serve warm with mild crackers or raw vegetables.

SPINACH WATER CHESTNUT DIP

Prepare 24 hours before serving.

1 package Knorr dry vegetable soup mix

1 cup sour cream

1 cup mayonnaise

1 can sliced water chestnuts, drained

1 package frozen chopped spinach, well drained and patted dry

Makes 3 to 3½ cups.

Mix all ingredients, adding spinach last. For best flavor, let sit in refrigerator 24 hours.

Serve in hollowed round loaf of sour dough, using bread pieces for dipping, or serve in hollowed purple cabbage with raw vegetables as dippers.

HATCH ROAD

A dip with refreshing taste and texture.

½ green pepper

2 hard cooked eggs

12 large stuffed olives

1 small onion

¼ pound bleu cheese, crumbled

3 ounces cream cheese

Serves 8 to 10.

Chop first 4 ingredients finely. Mix cheeses together. Thin, if necessary, with milk, cream or yogurt. Mix all ingredients together. Refrigerate.

Serve with raw vegetables presented in clusters on a nest of romaine, in a basket or other suitable container.

LAYERED NACHOS

1 (10-ounce) can Jalapeño bean dip

2 boxes frozen avocado dip

1 cup sour cream

½ cup mayonnaise

2 tablespoons dry taco seasoning

1 (4.2-ounce) can chopped black olives

1 tomato, chopped and seeded

1 bunch green onions, chopped

¾ pound Cheddar cheese, finely grated

1 pound round tortilla chips

Serves 12 generously.

Spread bean dip on plate or platter 9 inches in diameter. Spread thawed avocado dip over bean dip. Combine sour cream, mayonnaise and taco seasoning; spread over avocado. Layer olives, tomato, onions and cheese, in that order, over sour cream mixture.

May be refrigerated for 2 to 3 hours but best served at room temperature. Serve with tortilla chips.

HOT BEAN DIP

¼ pound sharp Cheddar cheese, grated

¼ pound Monterey Jack cheese, grated

1 can Frito Bean Dip or 1 (15-ounce) can refried beans

8 ounces cream cheese, softened

14 drops Tabasco sauce (or to taste)

4 green onions, chopped

1 cup sour cream

1 package taco seasoning mix

Tortilla chips

Serves 8 to 12.

Preheat oven to 350°. Combine Cheddar and Jack cheeses; set aside.

Mix remaining ingredients until well blended.

In the bottom of 1½ quart casserole spread layer of bean mixture; cover with layer of grated cheeses. Repeat, ending with cheeses.

Bake 25 to 30 minutes. Serve with tortilla chips.

CHILI CON QUESO

Serve in a chafing dish with corn chips.

2 pounds mild processed cheese, cubed (Velveeta)

1 medium onion, chopped fine

1 can green chiles, well drained and chopped

1 (16-ounce) can peeled tomatoes, drained and chopped (reserve the juice)

2 cloves garlic, minced fine

1 teaspoon garlic salt (or to taste)

Serves 12 generously.

Combine all ingredients in top of double boiler. Cook until cheese is melted and onions are tender. Add a little of the reserved tomato juice if mixture seems too thick. Place in chafing dish or heated bowl and serve.

CHILI CHEESE SQUARES

4 tablespoons butter or margarine

5 eggs

¼ cup flour

½ teaspoon baking powder

Dash salt

1 (4-ounce) can chopped green chiles

1 cup small curd cottage cheese

½ pound Monterey Jack cheese, shredded

Makes 3 dozen.

Preheat oven to 400°. Place butter in 9-inch square baking pan. Melt in oven, tipping pan to coat bottom.

In large bowl, beat eggs. Stir in flour, baking powder and salt. Add melted butter from baking pan but leave a light coating on bottom. Blend in chiles, cottage cheese and Jack cheese. Pour batter into pan. Bake 15 minutes. Reduce heat to 350° and bake 30 to 35 minutes longer or until lightly browned. Cool slightly and cut into small squares.

May be frozen; thaw before baking. Before serving, reheat in 400° oven for 10 minutes or until hot. Recipe may be doubled and baked in a 9 x 13-inch baking dish.

CONTINUOUS CHEESE CROCK

Should be made a week before serving so flavors will meld.

1 pound cheese, any combination, grated

½ pound butter (2 cubes), softened

¼ cup brandy, sherry, wine or beer

Dash Tabasco or cayenne

2 tablespoons Worcestershire sauce

Makes about 5 cups.

Combine cheeses and butter in food processor or large bowl of electric mixer; whip until light and fluffy. Add remaining ingredients. Pack into crocks and refrigerate.

To serve, bring to room temperature for easy spreading consistency. Serve with crackers or thin-sliced cocktail bread.

This mixture will freeze, and it keeps well in the refrigerator. Add ingredients as needed to replenish supply. The cheeses and beverages don't have to match.

PINEAPPLE CHEESE BALL

The green pepper flavor will surprise you.

2 (8-ounce) packages cream cheese, softened

2 cups pecans, chopped

1 (8½-ounce) can crushed pineapple, drained

¼ green pepper, finely chopped

2 tablespoons onion, finely chopped

1 teaspoon Johnny's seasoned salt

Makes 40 servings.

Beat cream cheese with a fork until smooth.

Gradually stir in half the nuts and remaining ingredients; shape into a ball and roll in remaining pecans. Wrap in plastic wrap; refrigerate until well chilled.

Serve with crackers.

CHUTNEY CREAM CHEESE

Your best chutney is a must.

1 (8-ounce) package cream cheese, softened

1 cup sharp Cheddar cheese, grated

¼ cup dry sherry

1 teaspoon curry powder

Chutney to spread over cheese

4 slices bacon, cooked, drained and crumbled

4 green onions, chopped

Dry-roasted peanuts, chopped (optional)

Shredded coconut (optional)

Serves 12 generously.

In mixing bowl or food processor, combine cheeses with sherry and curry powder. Pat into pie or quiche plate for serving. Spread chutney over top; refrigerate.

Before serving, sprinkle crumbled bacon and chopped onions over chutney. If desired, add a layer of chopped, dry-roasted peanuts or shredded coconut. Serve with crackers.

HAWAIIAN STUFFED LYCHEE NUTS

8 ounces cream cheese, softened

3 ounces crystalized ginger, finely chopped

2 (20-ounce) cans whole, seedless lychee nuts, well drained

Salad greens

1 jar macadamia nuts

Makes 48.

Combine cream cheese and ginger. Stuff mixture into lychee nuts with a small spoon. Chill.

Serve on a bed of greens. Just before serving, garnish each with one-half macadamia nut.

SAGANAKI

Greek flaming cheese.

1 pound Kasseri or Kefalotiri cheese

2 tablespoons butter, melted

2 tablespoons brandy

½ lemon

Serves 4 to 6.

Heat oven to broil. Have serving tray ready with crackers. lemon and brandy

Cut cheese into 3 wedges; arrange in star shape in a pie pan or shallow quiche pan suitable for broiling and serving. Pour melted butter over cheese. Broil 4 to 6 inches from heat until cheese is bubbly and light brown. Add to serving tray and take to guests.

Pour slightly warmed brandy over cheese and ignite immediately, in front of guests. Squeeze lemon juice over cheese to extinguish flame.

Serve at once with firm crackers, toasted pita bread or crusty French bread slices.

Mozzarella may be used as a substitute cheese if others are unavailable.

BRIE IN PUFF

A beautiful presentation.

1 pound Brie cheese round

1 (17¼-ounce) package puff pastry (2 sheets)

1 egg

1 tablespoon water

Serves 8.

Place Brie on one sheet of puff pastry. Top with second sheet and shape around the brie; trim. Seal pastry edges together with water; crimp firmly.

Wrap with plastic wrap, then with heavy duty foil. Seal tightly and freeze.

Brush frozen puff with a wash of egg and water beaten together with a fork.

Bake at 425° for 40 to 45 minutes or until golden brown. Let stand about 30 minutes before serving.

To cook without freezing, bake in 400° oven 35 to 40 minutes until golden; let stand before serving.

MINIATURE QUICHE LORRAINES

Easy gourmet.

3 ounces cream cheese, softened

½ cup butter (1 cube), softened

1 cup flour

6 slices bacon

1 cup onion, chopped

2 eggs, slightly beaten

¾ cup sour cream

½ teaspoon salt

Dash pepper

12 ounces Swiss cheese, grated

Makes 36 to 40.

Cream cheese and butter. Add flour and mix by hand. Press into miniature muffin pans.

Fry bacon until crisp; drain and crumble. Reserve 2 tablespoons drippings; add onion and cook until tender but not brown. Combine bacon, onion and remaining ingredients; spoon into the prepared shells. Bake in a preheated 375° oven for 20 to 30 minutes. Serve warm or at room temperature.

These freeze beautifully after baking.

RYE DIP

3 tubes Kraft nippy cheese

1¼ ounces Roquefort cheese

2 tablespoons soft butter

½ medium onion, grated

1 teaspoon Worcestershire sauce

½ to 1 cup beer, heated and cooled

1 round loaf rye or pumpernickel bread

Mix the cheeses, butter, onion and Worcestershire; blend well. Add cooled beer.

Hollow out center of bread. Pour dip into bread. Use the pieces of bread scooped from loaf to dip.

Julianne Phillips

Julianne Phillips

An actress who made her debut on the stage of Lake Oswego Community Theater. Now the wife of "The Boss", rock star Bruce Springsteen.

PHYLLO CHEESE ONION ROLLS

½ cup butter (1 cube)

3 large onions, thinly sliced

½ teaspoon salt

6 ounces cream cheese, softened

6 ounces Swiss cheese, shredded

½ teaspoon poppy seeds (optional)

½ pound phyllo dough

Makes about 5 dozen.

Melt 3 to 4 tablespoons of butter in a frying pan. Add onions and salt; cook over moderate heat until limp and golden brown. Remove from heat; add cream cheese, Swiss cheese and poppy seeds. Cool.

Follow package directions carefully to prevent drying of phyllo dough while working with it. Melt remaining butter. To make each cheese roll, stack 4 sheets of phyllo dough, brushing each layer lightly with melted butter, streaking rather than coating completely. Place ⅓ of onion mixture in an even band along the edge of one wide side of the 4-layer stack; roll snugly to enclose. Cut roll in half and place halves, seam side down, a few inches apart on buttered cookie sheet. Brush the entire surface with butter. Repeat with other 2 rolls. At this point rolls can be covered and chilled overnight.

Before baking, cut rolls in ¾-inch slices but leave in place. Bake in preheated 400° oven until golden, about 12 minutes if started at room temperature or 17 minutes if chilled. Cool slightly; separate and serve.

CHEESE-OLIVE PUFFS

15 min

1 (5-ounce) jar Kraft bacon-cheese spread

4 tablespoons butter or margarine

Dash Tabasco sauce

Dash Worcestershire sauce

¾ cup flour

30 stuffed green olives

Makes 30 puffs.

Blend cheese and butter until fluffy; use a food processor if possible. Add Tabasco and Worcestershire; stir in flour and mix well to form dough. Shape dough around well-drained olives (each ball will be about the size of a walnut). Bake at 400° for 12 to 15 minutes.

These freeze well. Freeze unbaked; thaw before baking.

makes about 38/39

PECAN CHEESE BITES

3½ cups flour

¼ teaspoon cayenne pepper

¼ teaspoon salt

1½ cups butter or margarine (3 cubes), softened

6 to 8 drops Worcestershire sauce

1 pound sharp Cheddar cheese, shredded

1½ cups pecan halves

Makes 6 dozen.

Sift flour, cayenne and salt into large bowl. Cut in butter and Worcestershire sauce with pastry blender until coarse crumbs form. Knead in cheese, one cup at a time, until mixture is no longer crumbly.

Shape into 1-inch balls. Press pecan half into each ball. Place 1 inch apart on ungreased cookie sheet. Bake at 375° 18 to 20 minutes or until lightly browned and set. Cool on wire rack. Serve warm or cold.

Unbaked balls may be frozen and baked when needed. Baked balls may be stored in airtight container for 2 to 3 days.

NORWEGIAN FLAT BREAD SNACK

1 cup butter (2 cubes)

1 cup Parmesan cheese, finely grated

¼ cup chopped parsley

2 teaspoons seasoned salt

Norwegian flat bread (20 to 30)

Makes 20 to 30 snacks.

Melt butter; add cheese, parsley and salt. Spread on flat bread with a pastry brush. Bake on cookie sheet for 3 to 4 minutes at 325°. While baking, leave oven door open, as these burn easily.

Adds a crisp texture when served with soups or salads.

SPANISH CHEESE SPREAD

1 pound Cheddar cheese, grated

½ cup or more stuffed green olives, chopped

1 (4-ounce) can green chiles, chopped

1 (8-ounce) can tomato sauce

½ cup salad oil

3 tablespoons vinegar

1 or 2 medium yellow onions, very finely chopped

1 to 2 cloves garlic, minced

7 to 10 dashes Worcestershire sauce

7 to 10 dashes Tabasco

Makes about 6 cups.

Combine all ingredients thoroughly. Spread on sliced bread and broil until bubbly and slightly browned.

To serve as an appetizer, spread on sliced cocktail bread; to serve as an accompaniment to soup or salad, use sliced French or sourdough bread.

LIVERWURST PÂTÉ

Toasted walnuts make the difference.

1 pound liverwurst or Braunschweiger, cut into cubes

1 pound low fat cottage cheese, drained

½ cup Best Foods mayonnaise

½ teaspoon prepared mustard

½ teaspoon thyme

½ teaspoon tarragon

½ cup chopped walnuts, toasted

Makes 5 cups.

Place all ingredients except nuts in food processor; beat until the cottage cheese is completely incorporated into the liver mixture and there are no white particles visible.

Add nuts and mix well by hand. Pack into bowl or mold. Serve with crackers.

Flavor is best if made a day ahead.

CHA SHUI

Chinese broiled pork tenderloin.

1 tablespoon sherry

2 tablespoons soy sauce

2 tablespoons sugar

½ teaspoon salt

½ teaspoon cinnamon

2 pounds pork tenderloin, cut into 2 long strips

Makes 60 thin slices.

Mix all ingredients except pork. Add meat and marinate for 2 hours in baking pan. Leave in marinade and cook under broiler for 1 hour, turning frequently. Cut into thin, diagonal slices. Serve with Chinese mustard, chutney or apple.

Beverly Sills

Beverly Sills

World reknowned operatic soprano; director of the New York City Opera.

CRAB-SHRIMP BOWL

You may be tempted to eat this by the spoonful.

1 can condensed mushroom soup, undiluted

8 ounces cream cheese

l envelope unflavored gelatin

3 tablespoons cold water

1 cup celery, chopped

2 green onions, white part only, chopped

¼ pound crab

¼ pound shrimp

1 cup mayonnaise

2 ounces pimento, well drained and finely chopped

1 to 2 tablespoons lemon juice

Serves 6 to 8.

Heat soup and cream cheese together; stir until smooth. Add gelatin softened in water. Mix and set aside to cool.

Add remaining ingredients and mix well. Spoon into serving bowl. Refrigerate until set; flavor improves overnight. Serve with crackers or chips.

SAYADIA TAHINI

Elegant presentation, yet deceptively simple to prepare. The Hummus Bi Tahini is an excellent dip as well as a topping for fish.

1 (15-ounce) can garbanzo beans, drained

⅓ cup lemon juice

4 tablespoons olive oil

¼ cup tahini (sesame paste)

½ teaspoon salt

1 cup clam nectar

1 cup white wine

6 tablespoons green onion, minced

2 pounds petrale sole fillets

Dash salt

Dash white pepper

¼ cup butter, melted

Serves 8 to 10.

To make Hummus Bi Tahini, combine first five ingredients in blender or food processor; mix well and taste for seasoning. Set aside.

Preheat oven to 350°. Simmer nectar and wine 5 to 10 minutes. Butter 10 x 14 inch baking dish; sprinkle with 3 tablespoons green onion. Salt and pepper fish; arrange half the fillets in baking dish, overlapping slightly. Brush with melted butter; sprinkle with remaining green onion. Arrange remaining fillets in second layer; brush with rest of butter. Pour enough wine and nectar liquid over fish to barely cover.

Cover fish with buttered wax paper; place in lower third of oven. Bake 10 minutes, just until fish becomes opaque; do not overcook. Cool in liquid. May be prepared to this point up to two days ahead and refrigerated.

Drain fish, then flake; add small amount Hummus Bi Tahini to bind and add flavor.

Place mixture on platter, form into curved fish shape. Or put into oiled fish mold; chill mixture to firm; dip mold in warm water to loosen; turn onto platter.

Spread fish form with Hummus Bi Tahini; decorate with pine nuts, black olive slices, bay shrimp, or whatever to resemble fins, scales, eyes.

CRAB PÂTÉ

½ pound picked crab

2 green onions, minced

1 tablespoon soft butter

1 sprig fresh parsley

1 tablespoon fresh lemon juice

½ cup homemade mayonnaise

Salt and pepper to taste

Serves 6.

Combine all ingredients and chill 2 hours before serving. Garnish with fresh parsley. Serve with thin rounds of bread or crackers.

MAYONNAISE

1 egg

1 teaspoon vinegar

½ teaspoon salt

¾ cup mild olive oil

¾ cup Saffola oil

Makes 1¾ cups.

Place egg, vinegar and salt in bowl of food processor; process for 30 seconds. With the machine running, add oils slowly.

Jane Hibler

Cookbook author and food columnist for The Oregonian.

CEVICHE

A palate refresher.

1 pound halibut, cut into ¼ to ½-inch cubes

Lime juice to cover fish

1 scant tablespoon salt

1 teaspoon oregano

½ teaspoon pepper

¼ teaspoon cloves

1 small onion, chopped

2 medium tomatoes, chopped

¼ cup chopped parsley

1 tablespoon olive oil

Dash or two Tabasco

Serves 6.

Cover cubes of fish with lime juice. Let stand 3 to 5 hours on counter, or overnight in refrigerator. Drain, rinse and pat dry with paper towels.

Mix remaining ingredients and toss with fish.

One pint bay scallops or 1 pound fresh, firm white fish filets may be substituted for the halibut.

SEAFOOD MOUSSE

⅓ cup tomato soup, undiluted

1 envelope unflavored gelatin

2 tablespoons cold water

1 (12-ounce) can tuna, crabmeat or shrimp

¼ cup celery, chopped

1 tablespoon lemon juice

¼ cup finely grated onion or thinly sliced green onions

½ cup mayonnaise

Dash Tabasco

Serves a crowd.

Heat tomato soup. Sprinkle gelatin over the water and let stand for 2 to 3 minutes. Add to soup, then cool.

Blend remaining ingredients in food processor; add to cooled soup. Pour into oiled fish or ring mold. Refrigerate at least 24 hours and up to 72.

Unmold and serve at room temperature with crackers. Mousse may be frozen.

Special
Effects

BEVERAGES

HOT SPICED TEA

3 quarts cold water

1 teaspoon whole cloves

1 cinnamon stick

6 tea bags

3 cups orange juice

1 cup lemon juice

1 cup sugar

Makes 24 (4-ounce) servings.

Combine water, cloves and cinnamon stick. Bring to boil and simmer 10 to 30 minutes. Add tea, steep seven minutes. Remove tea and spices, add orange juice, lemon juice and sugar. Heat to dissolve sugar. Serve hot.

SUNSHINES

1 part orange juice

1 part orange sherbet

Mix juice and sherbet in blender and serve.

ORANGE BLOSSOM FROSTS

Refreshing, light and nutritious.

1 (12-ounce) can frozen orange juice concentrate

1 (12-ounce) can cold water

1 cup powdered nonfat milk

½ teaspoon vanilla

1 or 2 eggs (optional)

Serves 8.

Beat ingredients together with a rotary beater or wire whisk; store in refrigerator. For each frost combine ½ cup of the prepared base and 1 cup crushed ice in a blender. Frappé until smooth and thick. Variations: Add ½ ripe banana or ½ fresh peach per serving; blend. Add sugar if desired.

PEACH NOG

1 large fresh peach or I cup canned peaches, sliced

1 egg

2 tablespoons honey or to taste

¼ cup orange juice

¼ cup powdered nonfat milk

1 tablespoon fresh lemon juice

⅛ teaspoon nutmeg, freshly grated

½ cup crushed ice

Makes 1 serving.

Whirl all ingredients in blender until smooth.

WEDDING PUNCH

Delicious and a favorite of caterers and brides. The bananas stay white.

1 (12-ounce) can frozen orange juice concentrate

1½ cups lemon juice

1 (46-ounce) can unsweetened pineapple juice

6 cups water

2 cups sugar

5 bananas, puréed in blender

5 quarts lemon-lime soda

85 to 90 (3-ounce) servings.

Combine all ingredients except soda. Pour into five one-pound coffee cans or comparable containers. Freeze.

When ready to serve, partially thaw; stir until mushy. Add soda just before serving, using 1 bottle of soda for each container of punch base.

MOCK MARGARITA PUNCH

A party drink that looks and tastes good but is "driveable"

1 (12-ounce) can frozen lemonade concentrate, thawed

1 (12-ounce) can frozen limeade concentrate, thawed

1 cup powdered sugar

4 egg whites

6 cups crushed ice

1 quart club soda, chilled

Lime slices

Coarse salt

24 (½ cup) servings.

In a 4-quart non-metal container, combine lemonade and limeade concentrates, powdered sugar, egg whites, and crushed ice. Mix well. Cover; freeze, stirring occasionally.

Remove container from freezer 30 minutes before serving. Spoon 2 cups of slush mixture into blender; add 1 cup club soda. Cover, blend until frothy.

To serve, rub rim of glass with lime slice and dip into coarse salt; fill glass. Garnish with lime slice.

Betty Brooks
Betty Brooks

Drama teacher and dynamic Lake Oswego Community Theater star and director.

STRAWBERRY ROSÉ PUNCH

A rosy color, a rosy glow.

2 (10-ounce) packages frozen sliced strawberries, thawed

½ cup sugar

2 fifths Rosé wine, chilled

1 (12-ounce) can frozen lemonade concentrate

1 fifth champagne or sparkling water, well chilled

Ice ring or ice cubes

30 (3-ounce) servings.

In a bowl combine strawberries, sugar and 2 cups of Rosé. Cover; let stand at room temperature 1 hour.

Strain mixture into punch bowl. Add frozen lemonade concentrate; stir until completely thawed. Add remaining Rosé and ice cubes or ice ring. Gently pour in champagne or sparkling water just before serving.

HOT BUTTERED RUM

Batter is always ready for one or many drinks.

2 cups butter (1 pound), softened

1 pound brown sugar

1 pound powdered sugar

2 tablespoons cinnamon

2 tablespoons nutmeg

1 quart French vanilla ice cream

Light rum or brandy

Cinnamon sticks

Makes about 2 quarts.

Combine first six ingredients and store in freezer.

For each drink place 2 tablespoons batter and 1½ ounces rum or brandy-rum combination in large mug or cup. Fill with boiling water; mix.

Serve with cinnamon stick.

MILK PUNCH

A great way to begin a brunch.

1¼ ounces brandy

3 ounces milk or half and half, very cold

1 teaspoon powdered sugar

Dash vanilla

Nutmeg

Serves 1.

Place all ingredients except nutmeg into a blender; mix thoroughly. Pour into an eight ounce glass; top with nutmeg.

Multiple of recipe may be made ahead and chilled.

GRAND MARNIER CHAMPAGNE COCKTAIL

Fresh fruit

Grand Marnier

Champagne

Prepare fresh fruit pieces, (strawberries, orange pieces, apricots, etc.).

For each drink, place one piece fruit in glass. Fill hollow stem of champagne glass with one tablespoon Grand Marnier. Fill glass with champagne.

BRIAN'S GOLDEN GIN FIZZ

1 tablespoon orange flower water

½ cup half and half

2 eggs

1 cup gin

4 ice cubes

¼ cup powdered sugar

½ cup lemon juice

Serves 4.

Place all ingredients in blender. Mix well until thick and frothy.

SHANDY GAFF

A true thirst quencher.

One part dark ale, chilled

One part lemonade, chilled

Mix and serve in frosted glasses.

Props

BREADS & CONSERVES

RICE HOT CAKES

Light and fluffy and delicious.

1 cup cooked rice

1 cup buttermilk

2 egg yolks, beaten

3 tablespoons vegetable oil

¼ teaspoon soda

¼ teaspoon salt

1 teaspoon sugar

1 teaspoon baking powder

1 cup minus 2 tablespoons flour, sifted

2 egg whites, stiffly beaten

Makes 13 to 18 cakes.

Combine rice, buttermilk and beaten egg yolks. Add oil. Sift dry ingredients; add to rice mixture. Fold in beaten egg whites.

Cook small or medium cakes on hot griddle until lightly browned on both sides. Serve with syrup or strawberry jam.

FINNISH PANCAKE

4 eggs

2¼ to 2½ cups milk

¼ cup honey

1 cup flour

½ teaspoon lemon extract

3 tablespoons butter or margarine

Powdered sugar

Serves 4 to 6.

Place first 5 ingredients in blender and mix until blended; scrape sides with spatula. Allow to stand for 30 minutes while oven preheats to 425°.

Melt 3 tablespoons butter in oven in 8 to 10-inch cast iron skillet. Blend mixture once more before pouring into hot skillet. Bake 25 minutes. When done, knife inserted into center will come out mostly clean.

Serve in pie shaped wedges with honey, maple syrup, or seasonal fruit or berries dusted with powdered sugar; fresh peaches are special.

GERMAN PANCAKE

The chilled pan helps the center of the pancake to puff up as dramatically as the sides.

3 eggs

½ cup flour

½ teaspoon salt

½ cup milk

2 tablespoons butter, melted

Serves 2 to 3.

Thickly butter bottom and sides of 9 or 10-inch heavy skillet or baking dish. Place in freezer for 10 to 15 minutes.

Beat eggs until well blended. Stir flour and salt together; add to eggs in 4 parts, beating after each just until smooth. Add milk in 2 parts, beating slightly after each. Beat in melted butter. Pour batter into cold skillet. Bake at 425° about 15 minutes; reduce heat to 375° and bake another 10 to 15 minutes.

For slightly larger pancake in same size pan, use 4 eggs, ⅔ cup flour, ½ teaspoon salt, ⅔ cup milk and 3 tablespoons melted butter.

Serve with melted butter, lemon juice and powdered sugar, or either of the following toppings.

SPICED APPLE TOPPING

3 tablespoons butter

3 tart apples, peeled, cored and thinly sliced

⅓ cup sugar

½ teaspoon cinnamon

¼ teaspoon nutmeg

Scant ⅛ teaspoon ground cloves

Makes 4 cups.

Melt butter in skillet; add apples. Combine sugar and spices; sprinkle on top. Slowly cook over low heat, turning occasionally until glazed and tender, about 10 minutes. Spoon onto center of the baked pancake and serve at once.

SWISS HONEY BUTTER TOPPING

½ cup butter (1 cube)

½ cup honey

½ cup whipping cream

1 teaspoon vanilla

Makes 1½ cups.

Cream butter and honey in small mixing bowl. Slowly add whipping cream, beating continuously until mixture is fluffy. Add vanilla. Spoon over hot pancakes as they are served.

OVERNIGHT YEAST WAFFLES WITH CINNAMON-BLUEBERRY SAUCE

2 cups flour

1 package active dry yeast

¼ teaspoon ground cardamom

2 cups milk

2 tablespoons butter or margarine

1 teaspoon sugar

1 teaspoon salt

2 eggs, separated

Makes 12 (4-inch) square waffles.

Combine flour, yeast and cardamom in large mixer bowl. In saucepan, heat milk, butter, sugar and salt just until warm, stirring constantly until butter almost melts. Add to flour mixture and beat at medium speed for 2 minutes, scraping sides of bowl repeatedly. Cover tightly and refrigerate overnight.

Just before baking, beat egg yolks with rotary beater until thick and lemon-colored, about 4 minutes. Stir into batter. Beat egg whites until stiff. Stir a small amount into batter to lighten, then gently fold in rest. Bake in preheated waffle iron.

If making and baking on same day, let batter stand loosely covered at room temperature for 1½ to 2 hours before adding eggs.

Serve with the following or any favorite waffle topping.

CINNAMON-BLUEBERRY SAUCE

½ cup sugar

4 teaspoons cornstarch

½ teaspoon grated lemon peel

¼ teaspoon cinnamon

1 (10-ounce) package frozen unsweetened blueberries, thawed

⅔ cup water

1 teaspoon lemon juice

Makes 2 cups.

Combine sugar, cornstarch, lemon peel and cinnamon in a small bowl; set aside. In sauce-pan, combine ½ cup of blueberries and water. Bring to a boil. Mash berries. Add sugar mixture and cook over medium heat, stirring constantly, until sauce thickens and bubbles. Add the remaining blueberries and lemon juice; simmer 3 to 5 minutes longer.

Delicious on pancakes, toast or ice cream too.

CRISPY WAFFLES

2 cups Bisquick

1 egg

½ cup vegetable oil

1⅓ cups club soda

Serves 4.

Combine all ingredients with a wire whip. Bake in a preheated waffle iron, oiled or sprayed with non-stick coating. Serve with maple syrup.

STICKY BUNS

1 package Rhodes frozen rolls

1 small package butterscotch pudding

Cinnamon to taste

½ cup brown sugar

½ cup butter (1 cube), melted

1 cup nuts, chopped

Serves 6 to 8.

Prepare the night before serving. Place frozen rolls in greased bundt pan or 9 x 13-inch pan. Sprinkle with pudding mix, cinnamon, and brown sugar; pour on melted butter; top with nuts. Cover with waxed paper and let rise overnight.

Next morning, bake at 325° for 25 minutes, then 300° for 15 minutes. Turn pan over onto platter before cool so caramel sauce is on top.

CINNAMON ROLL-UPS

Delicious and amazingly simple.

1 (22½-ounce) loaf thin white sandwich bread, crusts trimmed

1 (8-ounce) package cream cheese

1 to 1½ tablespoons mayonnaise

½ cup butter or margarine (1 cube), melted

1 teaspoon cinnamon

1 cup sugar

Makes 48.

Spread each slice of bread with cream cheese which has been softened with mayonnaise. Roll up in jelly roll fashion; cut each roll into thirds.

Melt butter or margarine in small saucepan. Combine sugar and cinnamon in small bowl.

Dip rolls into butter, coating thoroughly. Roll in sugar-cinnamon mixture, coating evenly. At this point rolls may be refrigerated or frozen.

Before serving, place under broiler. Broil until browned and bubbly, approximately 3 minutes.

NORTHWEST CINNAMON ROLLS

A prizewinner.

Dough:

3 packages yeast

1 cup water (105-115°)

2 teaspoons sugar

2 cups milk

1 cup sugar

1 teaspoon salt

1 cup butter (2 cubes), softened

6 eggs, beaten

9 to 10 cups flour

Filling:

½ cup butter (1 cube), melted

2 cups walnuts, chopped

1 pound brown sugar

4 teaspoons cinnamon

Frosting:

1 pound powdered sugar

½ cup butter (1 cube), softened

2 teaspoons rum or vanilla extract

Milk

Makes 24.

Dissolve yeast in water with 2 teaspoons sugar. Bring milk, butter, salt and sugar to a scald. Cool and add eggs. Add yeast. Add flour gradually and mix thoroughly; no need to knead. Cover with damp cloth and allow to rise 2 hours in warm place.

Dough will be sticky; add more flour until it can be worked. Divide dough into three portions; roll each into a rectangle 18 x 12 inches. Mix filling ingredients together; divide among each portion of dough. Roll; cut into 1½-inch slices. Place on greased baking sheet; let rise two hours.

Bake 10 minutes at 375° or until golden brown.

For frosting, mix powdered sugar, butter and flavoring; add milk in small amounts, just until smooth. Frost rolls while still warm.

DANISH APPLE PASTRY

Pastry:

2½ cups flour

1 teaspoon salt

1 cup shortening

1 egg yolk

Milk, enough to make ⅔ cup with egg yolk

Filling:

2 handfuls cornflakes, crushed

7 to 8 cups tart apples, sliced (8 to 10 apples)

1 cup sugar

1 teaspoon cinnamon

Topping:

1 egg white, beaten

Glaze:

1 cup powdered sugar

1 tablespoon water

1 teaspoon vanilla

Serves 15 to 20.

Preheat oven to 400°. Combine flour and salt. Cut in shortening to consistency of coarse crumbs. Separate egg; set white aside. Add milk to yolk; combine. Drizzle into pastry mix, tossing gently; gather into a ball. Divide in half. Roll out one half to fit 10½ x 15½-inch jelly roll pan.

Sprinkle with corn flakes; cover with apples. Combine sugar and cinnamon; sprinkle on apples.

Roll out second half of pastry and place on top; pinch edges to seal. Beat egg white until stiff and brush over top crust. Bake for 60 minutes.

Combine glaze ingredients and drizzle over warm pastry. Cut into bars.

ALMOND PASTRY

Crust:

2 cups flour

2 tablespoons water

1 cup butter (2 cubes), softened

Puff:

1 cup water

½ cup butter (1 cube)

1 cup flour

3 eggs

1 teaspoon almond extract

Frosting:

1 cup powdered sugar

½ teaspoon almond extract

1 tablespoon butter

1 tablespoon milk

Slivered almonds

Makes 2 pastries.

Place crust ingredients in food processor; process until ball is formed (a bit more flour may be needed). Divide dough in half; make 2 crusts by pressing each ball on cookie sheet to shape of 15 x 5 inches.

In a saucepan heat water and butter to boiling. Remove from heat and add flour; beat until smooth. Add eggs, one at a time, beating hard after each addition. Add almond extract. Divide in half and spread each half on a crust. Bake at 375° for 45 minutes.

Mix frosting ingredients and spread on warm pastries. Top with slivered almonds.

Serve at room temperature.

POPOVERS

Cold start, spectacular finish.

2 eggs, slightly beaten

1 cup milk

1 cup flour

1 teaspoon salt

1 teaspoon butter, melted

Makes 5.

Mix ingredients with whisk and pour into 5 standard pyrex custard cups which have been well greased, including the rims, with vegetable oil.

Place on cookie sheet in a cold oven. Set at 400° and bake for 1 hour or until golden.

CLOUD NINE BISCUITS

The highest, lightest biscuits imaginable.

2 cups flour

1 tablespoon sugar

4 teaspoons baking powder

½ teaspoon salt

½ cup shortening

1 egg, beaten

⅔ cup milk

Makes 20 to 24.

Sift dry ingredients together; cut in shortening until mixture resembles coarse crumbs. Combine egg and milk; add all at once to flour mixture. Stir with fork until dough is a soft mass. Turn onto lightly floured surface; knead gently with heel of hand, 15 to 20 strokes; dough will be rather moist. Roll to ¾ inch thickness. Cut in 2-inch squares or use a 2-inch biscuit cutter dipped in flour. Place on ungreased baking sheet, one inch apart. May chill at this point 1 to 3 hours before baking. Bake at 450° for 10 to 14 minutes or until golden brown.

For drop biscuits, increase milk to ¾ cup; omit kneading and cutting. Drop from tablespoon onto cookie sheet.

PUMPKIN DATE BREAD

4 cups sugar

4 cups flour

1 heaping teaspoon ground cloves

1 heaping teaspoon cinnamon

Dash allspice

Dash nutmeg

½ teaspoon salt, rounded

4 teaspoons baking soda

1 (29-ounce) can pumpkin

1 cup salad oil

2 cups broken walnuts or pecans

2 cups fresh dates, chopped

Makes 5 small loaves.

Preheat oven to 350°. Grease 7⅜ x 3⅝ x 2¼-inch loaf pans. Combine dry ingredients in large mixing bowl. Add pumpkin, oil, nuts, and dates; mix. Spoon into loaf pans, filling only ⅔ full. Bake one hour.

Batter may be used for muffins; bake 25 minutes.

Freezes well.

GLAZED LEMON LOAF

Moist and easy to make.

½ cup shortening

1 cup sugar

2 eggs, beaten

½ cup sour cream

Grated rind of 1 lemon

½ teaspoon salt

1½ cups flour

1 teaspoon baking powder

½ cup walnuts or pecans, chopped

2 tablespoons powdered sugar

Glaze:

1 cup powdered sugar

Juice of 1 lemon

Grated rind of 1 lemon

Makes 1 loaf.

Cream together shortening, sugar, eggs, sour cream and lemon rind. Combine salt, flour and baking powder; add to creamed mixture. Combine nuts and powdered sugar; set aside. Place half of batter in greased 5 x 9-inch loaf pan; sprinkle half of nut mixture over batter. Repeat.

Bake at 350° for 1 hour. While still warm, poke holes in top with toothpick and drizzle glaze over loaf. Cool in pan.

GRAPENUT LOAF

Delicious toasted too.

½ cup grapenuts cereal

1 cup milk

1 cup sugar

½ teaspoon baking soda

¼ teaspoon salt

1 teaspoon baking powder

2 cups flour

1 egg, slightly beaten

Makes 1 loaf.

Preheat oven to 375°. Soak grapenuts in milk for 1 hour in mixing bowl.

Line a 9 x 5-inch bread pan with waxed paper.

Sift dry ingredients together; add to grapenut mixture. Blend in egg. Spoon into bread pan. Bake for 40 to 45 minutes or until done. Remove from pan; immediately wrap in damp towel to steam.

ORANGE CRANBERRY BREAD

2 cups flour

1 cup sugar

½ teaspoon baking soda

½ teaspoon baking powder

Juice and grated rind of 1 large orange.

2 tablespoons vegetable oil

Hot water

1 egg

½ cup chopped walnuts

1 cup raw cranberries, halved

Makes 1 standard loaf or 2 small loaves.

Preheat oven to 350°. Sift dry ingredients together into large mixing bowl.

Put orange juice and rind in one-cup measuring cup; add oil, then hot water to the ¾ cup mark.

Beat egg in a small bowl. Add small amount of hot juice mixture to warm egg gradually, then beat in remainder. Stir into dry ingredients, blending thoroughly. Gently fold in nuts and cranberries.

Spoon into one greased and floured 9 x 5 x 3-inch loaf pan or two small pans. Bake 1¼ hours or until golden brown. Adjust baking time for smaller loaves.

OREGON PRUNE BREAD

2 cups boiling water

2 cups dried prunes, pitted and chopped

2 teaspoons baking soda

2 tablespoons butter, melted

1¼ cups sugar

1 egg

1 teaspoon vanilla

4 cups flour, sifted

2 teaspoons baking powder

1 teaspoon salt

1 cup walnuts, chopped

Makes 2 loaves.

Preheat oven to 300°. Pour boiling water over uncooked prunes. Add soda; allow to stand while mixing batter.

Cream butter, sugar and egg; stir in vanilla. Sift dry ingredients together. Add to creamed mixture alternately with water from prunes. Stir in prunes and nuts. Spoon into two greased 5 x 9-inch loaf pans. Bake for 1 hour. Chill. Serve thinly sliced with cream cheese.

PINEAPPLE ZUCCHINI BREAD

3 eggs

1 cup oil

1 cup sugar

2 teaspoons vanilla

3 cups flour

1 teaspoon salt

½ teaspoon baking powder

2 teaspoons baking soda

1½ teaspoons cinnamon

¾ teaspoon nutmeg

1 cup walnuts, finely chopped

1 cup currants

2 cups zucchini, seeded and coarsely shredded

1 (8-ounce) can crushed pineapple

Makes 2 loaves.

Preheat oven to 350°. Beat eggs well; add oil, sugar and vanilla. Beat until thick and foamy.

Combine dry ingredients, nuts and currants. Stir zucchini and well-drained pineapple into egg mixture. Stir in dry ingredients until just blended; do not beat.

Divide batter evenly and spoon into two greased and floured 5 x 9-inch loaf pans. Bake for 1 hour or until done.

BLUEBERRY MUFFINS

You can't eat just one.

2 cups blueberries

2⅓ cups flour

1 cup sugar

2 teaspoons cream of tartar

1 teaspoon baking soda

½ teaspoon salt

6 tablespoons butter

1 egg, lightly beaten

¾ cup milk

½ teaspoon vanilla

Makes 20 to 24.

Preheat oven to 350°. Toss blueberries with ⅓ cup of the flour and set aside.

Sift remaining flour and rest of dry ingredients together into large bowl. Cut in butter with pastry blender until mixture resembles meal.

In another bowl combine egg, milk and vanilla. Add to dry ingredients and stir just until moistened. Fold in blueberries. Spoon batter into greased or paper-lined muffin cups, filling about ⅔ full. Bake 20 to 30 minutes or until golden brown.

Muffins freeze well; reheat before serving.

MINIATURE ORANGE MUFFINS

1 cup sugar

½ cup orange juice

Muffins:

½ cup butter (1 cube)

1 cup sugar

¾ cup sour cream or plain yogurt

2 cups flour

1 teaspoon baking soda

1 teaspoon salt

Grated rind of one orange

½ cup raisins

½ cup walnuts, chopped

Makes 4 dozen.

Preheat oven to 375°. Mix sugar and juice. Set aside for dipping after muffins are baked.

Cream together butter and sugar. Add sour cream or yogurt alternately with sifted dry ingredients. Fold in orange rind, raisins and nuts. Batter will be stiff.

Use miniature muffin pans, either well greased or sprayed with non-stick coating. Fill no more than half full. Bake 12 to 15 minutes.

While still warm, dip each muffin in the orange juice-sugar mix. Cool on wire rack.

RAZUDAN MUFFINS

Batter is always ready in your refrigerator for baking fresh muffins in a jiffy.

2 cups boiling water

2 cups quick cooking oatmeal

2 cups all-bran cereal

2 cups shredded wheat, crushed

1 cup vegetable oil

3 cups sugar

4 eggs

1 quart buttermilk

5 cups flour

1 tablespoon salt

5 teaspoons baking soda

Makes 3 quarts batter.

Pour boiling water over oatmeal, all-bran and shredded wheat. Let stand without stirring for 20 minutes or until lukewarm.

In large mixing bowl, combine oil and sugar; add eggs and buttermilk; blend. Combine flour, salt and baking soda; add to egg mixture. Blend. Pour cereal mixture into flour mixture and blend gently; do not beat.

Covered batter keeps in refrigerator for 3 months. Muffins may be baked as needed. Bake at 350° for 25 to 30 minutes.

Variations: add raisins, chopped dates, or nuts or grated orange peel, or top with cinnamon and sugar.

MAPLE CRUMB MUFFINS

Best fresh from the oven.

2 cups flour

2 teaspoons baking powder

½ teaspoon salt

1 egg, beaten

½ cup sour cream

¾ cup maple syrup

Streusel topping:

¾ cup flour

¼ cup sugar

4 tablespoons butter

Makes 12.

Preheat oven to 400°. Sift flour, baking powder, and salt into mixing bowl. Stir in egg, sour cream, and syrup; do not overmix. Spoon into well-greased or paper-lined muffin cups, filling ⅔ full.

Combine flour and sugar; cut in butter. Sprinkle over muffin batter. Bake 20 to 25 minutes or until golden brown. Serve warm.

SWEDISH SCORPA BREAD

Crisp, flavorful loaves.

1 quart whole milk

1 cup shortening and butter, softened

1 tablespoon salt

1 cup sugar

2 packages yeast

½ cup warm water (105-115°)

2 eggs, beaten

12 cups flour, sifted and divided in half

Makes 4 loaves.

In saucepan scald milk just until small bubbles appear around edge. Place shortening, salt and sugar in a very large bowl. Add hot milk; stir to melt shortening and dissolve sugar. Cool to lukewarm.

Sprinkle yeast over warm water in a small bowl or measuring cup; let stand 5 minutes.

Add eggs and yeast to lukewarm milk; stir to combine. Add 6 cups flour a little at a time, beating vigorously after each addition. Sprinkle a little flour on top; cover and let rise 1 to 2 hours or until doubled in bulk.

Add remaining flour a cup at a time, beating well. Work with hands when too stiff to beat; add more flour if sticky. Again, sprinkle a little flour on top, cover, and let rise 1 to 2 hours.

Punch down, then turn dough onto floured board and knead until smooth and elastic, at least 10 minutes. Form into 4 loaves. Place in greased 5 x 9 inch bread pans; cover and let rise again.

Bake in preheated 325 to 350° oven for 20 to 30 minutes. Sugar and cinnamon may be sprinkled on top of loaves before baking. For a crisp toast like zweibach, slice and dry in a slow oven.

LIMPA BREAD

1½ cups warm water (110 to 115°)

1 tablespoon dry yeast

2 cups sifted rye flour

1 cup warm water

½ cup molasses

1 tablespoon dry yeast

1 tablespoon salt

2 tablespoons melted butter or oil

Rind of 2 or 3 oranges, finely grated

1 teaspoon anise seed, crushed

2 cups sifted rye flour

1½ to 2 cups sifted all-purpose flour

1 egg

1 tablespoon water

Makes 2 or 3 loaves.

Combine first 3 ingredients and let sit, covered, at room temperature for one or two days, stirring once or twice.

With a wooden spoon, stir down the above sponge and add remaining ingredients except all-purpose flour, egg and water. Beat well. Add enough all-purpose flour, one cup at a time, to make a firm dough. When dough is too heavy to beat, turn onto lightly floured board and knead until smooth and elastic, adding more flour if necessary.

Place ball of dough in oiled bowl, turning to coat top of dough with oil. Cover with waxed paper, wrap in a towel, place in warm, draft-free place and allow to rise until doubled. Punch dough down, knead a bit to distribute bubbles, re-wrap and let rise again. Punch down and knead again. Shape into 2 or 3 oval loaves. Place on a greased baking sheet; cover and let rise until doubled.

Beat egg with tablespoon of water; brush glaze on loaves. Make 5 or 6 diagonal cuts, ¼ to ½ inch deep, on tops of loaves. Bake at 350° about 45 minutes or until brown. Bottom of loaves should sound hollow when tapped lightly. Cool on rack. Store in airtight bags or wrap snugly and freeze.

BAKED CHEESE FINGERS

1 (1-pound) loaf unsliced day old bread

1 (5-ounce) jar Kraft Old English Cheese Spread

½ cup (1 cube) plus 1 tablespoon margarine

Makes 32 fingers or 36 cubes.

Remove crusts from bread, then cut into fingers about 4 x ¾ x ¾ inches, or cubes of 1½ inches.

Melt cheese and margarine together in frying pan. Dip bread pieces in cheese mixture, turning to coat with a thin layer. Bake on well greased cookie sheet at 350° for about 10 minutes; watch so they don't burn.

GAMMY'S COFFEE CAN BREAD

Makes wonderful toast.

1 package active yeast

½ cup warm water

3 tablespoons sugar

⅛ teaspoon ground ginger

1 (13-ounce) can evaporated milk

1 teaspoon salt

2 tablespoons salad oil

4 to 4½ cups sifted flour

Butter or margarine

Makes one loaf.

Dissolve yeast in water in large bowl. Blend in 1 tablespoon sugar and ginger. Let stand in warm place until bubbly, approximately 15 minutes. Stir in 2 tablespoons sugar, milk, salt and salad oil.

With mixer on low speed, beat in flour, 1 cup at a time, beating well after each addition. Beat last cup of flour in with heavy spoon; keep adding flour until very stiff but too sticky to knead. Place in well-greased 2-pound coffee can. Cover with greased plastic lid. Freeze.

To thaw, let stand in warm place until lid pops off, usually 6 to 8 hours. Bake at 350° for 60 minutes. Crust should be very brown. Brush top with butter or margarine. Let cool slightly and then loosen and remove from pan. Finish cooling on rack.

CHEESE SPREAD

2 cups butter or margarine (1 pound), softened

¾ pound sharp Cheddar cheese, grated

¼ pound Romano cheese, grated

1 teaspoon garlic powder

1 teaspoon paprika

1 tablespoon Worcestershire sauce

Makes 6 cups.

Beat all ingredients together in mixer until fluffy. Store in refrigerator to use as desired; return to room temperature for ease in spreading.

Spread on sliced French bread or rolls. Bake at 350° 10 minutes or until bubbly. If using for appetizers, spread on small slices of bread such as cocktail loaf.

SAVORY BREAD

1 cup butter (2 cubes), or ½ cup butter and ½ cup margarine

½ teaspoon salt

1 teaspoon dried thyme leaves (not powder)

½ teaspoon dried savory leaves (not powder)

1 clove garlic, pressed

Generous amount paprika (optional)

Makes enough spread for a 2 pound loaf.

Cream butter and seasonings thoroughly. Store in refrigerator or freezer to use as desired. Soften before using so mixture can be spread thinly.

Use on sliced French bread or rolls, or on small cocktail loaves (rye with caraway is excellent). Wrap in foil. When ready to bake, turn foil back to avoid steaming. Bake at 375° for 45 minutes.

UNION JACK BREAD

1 loaf French bread

½ cup butter (1 cube), melted

¼ cup Parmesan cheese, grated

Monterey Jack cheese, cut into small cubes

Makes one loaf.

Make a lengthwise slice, at least ½ inch deep, down middle of loaf; do not cut through bottom crust. Next make 1-inch thick crosswise slices. Place loaf on a large piece of foil for baking.

Combine butter and Parmesan cheese; spread between slices. Insert Monterey Jack cheese into slits. Bring foil up around sides, but do not cover top. Bake at 475° for 7 to 8 minutes.

ONION CORN BREAD

Excellent flavor and contrast of textures.

4 tablespoons margarine

1½ cups onion, chopped

1 cup Cheddar cheese, grated and divided

1 cup sour cream

½ teaspoon salt

1 package Jiffy Cornmeal Muffin Mix

1 cup cream style corn

½ cup milk

1 egg, beaten

Makes 9 servings.

Preheat oven to 400°. Melt margarine in skillet. Add onions and cook slowly for 10 minutes; set aside to cool 5 to 10 minutes. Add ½ cup grated cheese, sour cream and salt; set aside.

Combine muffin mix, corn, milk and egg. Let sit for 2 minutes; pour into greased 8 x 8-inch pan. Gently spoon onion mixture over corn mixture. Sprinkle remaining cheese over top. Bake 30 to 40 minutes or until bubbly and golden brown. Let cool; cut into squares.

CONSERVES

PEACH CONSERVE

3 pounds peaches, peeled and chopped; save 2 or 3 peach pits

2 oranges, unpeeled and thinly sliced

1 (6-ounce) jar maraschino cherries, drained and sliced (reserve liquid)

6¾ cups sugar

½ teaspoon salt

1 (20-ounce) can crushed pineapple

Makes 7 (12-ounce) jars.

Crack peach pits and remove kernels.

Combine peaches, sliced oranges, juice from cherries, sugar, salt and peach kernels in sauce pan. Boil hard for 30 minutes, stirring occasionally. Add cherries and pineapple, including pineapple juice. Continue cooking until syrup is thick. Pour into sterilized jars and seal while hot.

PFLAUMENMUSS

A conserve.

1 pound dried pitted prunes

2 cups water

1 pound sugar

1 teaspoon ground cinnamon

½ teaspoon ground cloves

½ teaspoon ground ginger

Dash nutmeg

2 teaspoons cornstarch

Makes 1 quart.

Grind prunes with meat grinder; set aside. Bring water to boil in heavy pot. Add sugar, spices and prunes. Bring to a boil and boil slowly for 10 minutes, stirring constantly. Add cornstarch dissolved in a little cold water. Remove from heat and pour into container. Cool, then refrigerate.

Horst Mager

Portland restauranteur and "AM Northwest" guest chef.

RHUBARB RAISIN CONSERVE

3 pounds rhubarb, chopped in 1-inch lengths (frozen rhubarb may be used)

¼ cup water

1½ to 2 cups raisins

½ teaspoon salt

½ teaspoon nutmeg

½ teaspoon cinnamon

1 to 1½ cups sugar

½ cup brown sugar

2 envelopes unflavored gelatin

½ cup cold water

Red food coloring (optional)

Makes 3 quarts.

Cook rhubarb in water, stirring constantly to mash up chunks. Add raisins and salt; cook slowly until evenly textured. Add spices and sugars, then gelatin which has been softened in cold water. Cook, stirring, until gelatin and sugars are dissolved. If a rosier color is desired, add a few drops of red food coloring. Store in refrigerator. Keeps well, is the consistency of jam and is wonderful for breakfast on crisp hot buttered toast.

Stock

Characters

SOUPS

VICHYSSOISE

6 large leeks

2 large potatoes

6 cups chicken stock

1 teaspoon salt

1 teaspoon white pepper

½ teaspoon nutmeg

3 tablespoons chives, chopped

1 tablespoon lemon juice

1 cup heavy cream

2 tablespoons sour cream

1 tablespoon minced fresh parsley

Serves 4 to 6.

Using only the white part of the leeks, remove root ends and wash carefully; mince.

Peel potatoes and slice thinly. Simmer leeks and potatoes in the chicken broth until tender, about 30 minutes. Purée mixture in blender or food mill. Add remaining ingredients except sour cream and parsley. Chill.

Prior to serving, chill soup bowls. Ladle soup into bowls and garnish each with a dollop of sour cream and parsley.

GAZPACHO BLANCO

Wonderful for a picnic.

3 medium cucumbers,
   peeled and cut in chunks

3 cloves garlic

3 cups chicken broth

3 cups sour cream

Salt

White pepper

Makes 2 quarts.

Whirl cucumbers and garlic in blender until smooth. Add chicken broth, a little at a time, until smooth. Mix with sour cream and salt and pepper to taste.

Serve with condiments such as diced tomatoes, croutons, sliced green onions, diced avocado, bacon crumbles and chives.

GAZPACHO

Attractive and simple to prepare.

1 can condensed tomato soup

16 ounces tomato sauce

1 to 2 tablespoons olive oil

Dash Tabasco

2 tablespoons lemon juice

2 tablespoons wine vinegar

1 teaspoon garlic salt or 2 fresh cloves, mashed

⅛ teaspoon cayenne pepper

1 avocado, chopped

1 medium tomato, chopped

½ cup cucumber, sliced

1 small can black olives, sliced

½ cup green onion, sliced

½ cup green pepper, chopped

¼ cup minced parsley

Salt

Fresh garlic

10 ounces cooked shrimp (optional)

Fresh lemon

Sour cream (optional)

Serves 5.

Combine first 8 ingredients. Add vegetables and salt to taste. Chill at least 4 hours.

Rub each soup bowl with cut garlic bud, place shrimp in bowl and sprinkle with lemon. Add soup. Serve cold with a dollop of sour cream.

CHILLED ZUCCHINI SOUP

A refreshing start to a summer meal.

½ cup butter (1 cube)

4 cups onion, coarsely chopped

3 pounds zucchini, unpared, cut into 1-inch cubes

4 cups chicken broth

1 small clove garlic, minced

1 teaspoon salt

¼ teaspoon pepper

1 pint sour cream

½ to ¾ cup mayonnaise

1 teaspoon curry powder

Dash powdered ginger

1 tablespoon lemon juice

1 teaspoon sugar

Serves 10 to 12.

Melt butter in 7-quart stockpot. Add onions; cook, stirring often, until golden. Add zucchini; cook 5 to 10 minutes. Add chicken broth, garlic, salt and pepper. Bring to a boil, cover and simmer for 10 to 15 minutes; zucchini should be tender but not mushy. Purée in food processor or blender. Chill thoroughly (may be frozen at this stage).

When ready to serve, add remaining ingredients. Serve ice cold.

CREAM OF ASPARAGUS SOUP

An excellent recipe which takes advantage of fresh asparagus.

1 pound fresh asparagus

3½ cups chicken broth

4 tablespoons butter or margarine

¼ cup flour

½ cup half and half

¼ to ½ teaspoon salt

⅛ teaspoon pepper

Serves 6 to 8.

Trim asparagus and cut into 1-inch pieces. Cook until tender, 12 to 15 minutes, in 1 cup of chicken broth. Melt butter in deep saucepan. Remove from heat and stir in flour. Gradually add remaining broth and cook, stirring, until slightly thickened. Add cream, seasonings and cooked asparagus. Heat through. Taste and correct seasoning.

SCANDINAVIAN SWEET SOUP

A traditional first course at Christmas. You might also try it as dessert with rum or sherry added, drizzled over pound cake.

2½ cups water

½ teaspoon salt

1 cup sugar

1 stick cinnamon

Orange slices

Lemon slices

1 cup seedless raisins

1 can prunes or Italian plums

1 package frozen raspberries

½ cup minute tapioca (or a cornstarch and water paste)

Serves 6.

Combine ingredients; simmer about 30 minutes. (If using cornstarch and water paste, add after ingredients have finished simmering.)

Serve hot or cold. This soup is better if it sits for at least 6 hours. Just before serving remove cinnamon stick and add additional thin slices of oranges and lemons.

FLORENTINE SOUP

Wonderfully delicious hot or cold.

1 (10-ounce) package frozen chopped
  spinach

1 (8-ouhce) package cream cheese, room
  temperature

1 medium onion, chopped

1 cup fresh mushrooms, sliced

2 tablespoons butter or margarine

1 tablespoon flour

½ teaspoon salt

⅛ to ¼ teaspoon garlic powder or 1 clove
  fresh garlic, mashed

⅛ teaspoon white pepper

Dash nutmeg

3¼ cups milk

Serves 4 to 6.

Cook spinach just enough to thaw; drain well
and set aside. Soften cream cheese in a small
bowl and set aside.

In a 3-quart saucepan, sauté onion and mushrooms slowly in butter until tender but not
brown.

Add flour and seasonings to onion mixture; stir
over low heat for 1 to 2 minutes. Add milk and
cook over medium heat, stirring constantly, until
it starts to bubble.

Pour a little of the milk mixture into the softened
cream cheese and stir vigorously until smooth.
Add cheese and spinach to soup; stir until
cheese melts. Taste and adjust seasoning.

SPICY SAUSAGE AND CORN CHOWDER

A homey, flavorful, old fashioned kind of soup.

¼ pound or more Kielbasa, or 2 mild Italian sausages

2 tablespoons butter or margarine.

1 onion, chopped

2 potatoes, peeled and diced

1½ cups water

1 (16-ounce) can cream style corn

1 (4-ounce) can diced green chiles

½ teaspoon garlic powder

1 teaspoon salt

2 to 3 cups milk

Pepper to taste

Serves 4.

Cut sausage into cubes or crumble. Sauté lightly. Remove grease and set sausage aside.

Sauté onion in butter. Add potatoes and water; cook, covered, until vegetables are tender. Add corn, chiles and seasonings; simmer about 5 minutes. Add milk (amount depends on thickness desired); heat but do not boil. Taste and adjust seasonings.

BARNARDI MINESTRONE

Robust and hearty for a Sunday supper.

¼ pound bacon, minced

¼ pound ham, chopped

¼ pound Italian sausage, chopped

2 cloves garlic, crushed

1 onion, chopped

2 stalks celery, chopped and sliced

1 zucchini, sliced

1 leek, sliced

2 quarts beef stock

2 cups shredded cabbage

1 cup Italian red wine

1 (16-ounce) can red kidney beans

1 (28-ounce) can tomatoes

½ cup elbow macaroni

¼ cup fresh basil, chopped, or 1 tablespoon dry

Salt and pepper to taste

Pinch allspice

Oregano and dill (optional)

Parmesan cheese, grated

Serves 6 to 8.

Lightly brown meats in a heavy skillet. Add garlic, onion, celery, zucchini and leek. Cover and simmer 10 minutes.

Heat beef stock in large stockpot. Add contents of skillet, cabbage, wine and beans. Simmer, covered, 45 minutes.

Cut up tomato chunks with a pair of kitchen shears while they're still in the can. Add tomatoes and macaroni to the soup. Cover and cook 15 minutes longer. Add seasonings and herbs to taste.

Soup may be thinned with additional bouillon, tomato juice or wine. Sprinkle each serving with grated Parmesan cheese.

ZUCCHINI SOUP WITH BACON

Easy preparation; corn bread and salad complete the menu.

2 slices bacon, chopped

1½ pounds fresh zucchini

1 small onion, chopped

⅔ cup condensed consommé, undiluted

1⅓ cups water

½ teaspoon basil

1 small clove garlic, mashed

2 teaspoons chopped parsley

½ teaspoon salt

⅛ teaspoon pepper

½ teaspoon seasoning salt

Grated Parmesan cheese

Serves 4 to 6.

Sauté bacon in large saucepan. Wash zucchini, remove ends and cut into 1-inch chunks. Place in saucepan with bacon and remaining ingredients except cheese. Cover; cook until zucchini is just tender. Cool slightly.

Whirl mixture in blender, about 2 cups at a time, until smooth. Reheat soup if necessary.

Sprinkle cheese over each serving.

SPLIT PEA SOUP

1 pound split peas

3 quarts water

1½ teaspoons salt

2½ tablespoons butter

2 cups carrots, chopped

1½ cups sweet potatoes or yams, chopped

1½ cups onion, chopped

1 cup celery, chopped

¾ teaspoon marjoram

1 teaspoon basil

3 cloves garlic, minced

½ teaspoon ground cumin

Freshly ground black pepper to taste

Serves 8 to 12.

Place peas, water and salt in a large kettle and bring to a boil; lower heat and simmer for 1 hour. Skim off and discard foam. Sauté vegetables in butter approximately 10 minutes; add herbs and cook another 5 to 10 minutes. Add vegetables to peas and water; simmer, stirring occasionally, for 45 to 60 minutes. Ladle approximately half of the soup into blender and purée, then return it to kettle for a thickened, hearty, nourishing soup.

Lindsay Wagner

Lindsay Wagner

Oregon's own Bionic Woman; star of stage, screen and television.

OVEN-BAKED SPLIT PEA SOUP

The aroma fills the kitchen; the turnip adds a subtle sweetness.

1 pound ham hocks

1 cup green split peas

1 large turnip, peeled and quartered

1 large carrot, peeled and cut in large chunks

1 large onion, sliced

1 stalk celery, cut in chunks

1 bay leaf

2 cloves garlic, mashed

2 quarts water

¼ teaspoon white pepper

Salt to taste

Serves 6 to 8.

Combine all ingredients except salt in Dutch oven and bring to a boil. Place in 225° oven and bake, uncovered, 12 to 14 hours or until vegetables are soft and soup is somewhat thickened. Cool to room temperature. Remove bay leaf.

Remove ham from bones and set aside. Purée vegetables and broth in blender. Return to stockpot; add ham. Taste and correct seasoning, adding salt and pepper as desired. If a thinner consistency is desired, add chicken broth or milk and reheat to serve.

SPICY LENTIL SOUP

This has gusto—serve it with German beer and heavy rye bread.

1 (16-ounce) package lentils

1 garlic clove, mashed

1 onion, chopped

1 stalk celery, chopped

1 carrot, chopped

4 tomatoes, chopped

6 cups beef stock

1½ tablespoons vinegar

1 teaspoon paprika

1 teaspoon salt

½ teaspoon pepper

½ teaspoon thyme

1 large Kielbasa, cut into quarters

2 cups Burgundy wine

Fresh parsley, chopped

Serves 8 to 10.

Put all ingredients except wine and parsley into stockpot. Simmer ½ hour or more. Add wine and simmer another ½ hour. Before serving, top each bowl with fresh parsley. The longer this cooks, the thicker it becomes.

PLAZA III'S STEAK SOUP

A Kansas City special.

1 pound ground beef steak

½ cup butter (1 cube)

½ cup flour

4 (10-ounce) cans beef consommé

½ cup carrots, diced

½ cup celery, diced

½ cup onion, diced

1 (8-ounce) can tomatoes, chopped

1½ teaspoons Kitchen Bouquet

2 beef bouillon cubes

½ teaspoon black pepper

1 teaspoon MSG (optional)

1 (10-ounce) package frozen mixed
  vegetables

Serves 8.

Brown ground beef in stockpot. Remove meat with slotted spoon and set aside. Drain off all fat, leaving the brown particles in the pan. Add butter, melt, and add flour; stir to form a smooth paste. Cook over medium heat, without browning, for 3 minutes. Add consommé; cook, stirring constantly, until smooth and lightly thickened. Bring to a boil; add the fresh vegetables and seasonings with the tomatoes. Allow soup to regain the boil, then reduce heat and simmer, covered, for 30 minutes or until fresh vegetables are almost tender. Add frozen vegetables and browned beef; simmer an additional 15 minutes.

Serve with giant oyster crackers.

CHEESE SOUP

This is a favorite of four of our testers.

1 cup celery, chopped

1 cup onion, chopped

1 cup green pepper, chopped

1 cup carrots, chopped

2 cups chicken stock

1 cup butter (2 cubes)

⅔ cup flour

1 teaspoon salt

1 quart whole milk

1 quart nonfat milk

1 (16-ounce) jar Cheez Whiz

Serves 10.

Cook vegetables in chicken stock until tender; purée.

Melt butter in large saucepan; add flour and salt. Cook over low heat, stirring, for several minutes. Add milk slowly, stirring constantly, and cook until thickened, taking care to avoid scorching. Add cheese and blend well. Add the puréed vegetables and heat thoroughly without boiling.

CHICKEN BISQUE

This rich soup takes time to prepare but it's worth every minute.

3 pounds chicken

4 stalks celery, diced

4 carrots, peeled and diced

3 onions, diced

3 teaspoons salt

4 quarts water

1 cup butter (2 cubes)

¾ cup flour

8 to 10 drops yellow food coloring

1 teaspoon MSG (optional)

1 teaspoon pepper

1½ teaspoons Aromat by Knorr, or 1½ teaspoons Spice Island Chicken Seasoned Stock Base

1 tablespoon dry parsley

Serves 10 to 12.

Place chicken, vegetables, salt and water in large kettle. Cook on medium heat until chicken is tender and pulls away from bone, 45 to 60 minutes.

Remove chicken from liquid. Discard skin and bones; cut chicken into small pieces. Strain stock, reserving vegetables; return stock to kettle.

Make a roux by melting butter in small saucepan, then slowly adding flour and stirring until smooth.

Bring chicken stock to a low boil and slowly add roux, stirring constantly with a wire whisk. Simmer 15 minutes. Add food coloring, MSG, pepper, Aromat, parsley, chicken and vegetables.

SHERRIED CRAB SOUP

Elegant and exceedingly quick; perfect for the beach when you don't want to fuss.

1 can condensed tomato soup

1 can condensed beef bouillon

1 can condensed cream of mushroom soup

1 cup half and half

1 cup crab meat

Dry sherry to taste

Serves 6.

Combine soups and cream; heat slowly, taking care not to burn; do not boil. Add crab and sherry and heat through.

BAY SCALLOP CHOWDER

A sophisticated, subtly seasoned chowder.

3 medium potatoes, peeled and diced

1 small carrot, chopped

1 medium onion, chopped

2 cups chicken broth

½ teaspoon salt

¼ teaspoon ground pepper

1 small bay leaf

½ teaspoon thyme

½ pound fresh mushrooms, sliced

2 tablespoons butter

1 pound fresh bay scallops

½ cup dry white wine

1 cup whipping cream or half-and-half

1 egg yolk, beaten

Chopped fresh parsley

Paprika

Serves 4 to 5.

Combine vegetables, broth and seasonings in saucepan and simmer until tender. Remove bay leaf; place rest in blender and whirl until smooth.

Sauté mushrooms in butter; add scallops and wine and cook for 1 minute. Combine beaten egg yolk and cream; stir into scallop mixture. Add puréed vegetables; heat but do not boil. Serve sprinkled with parsley and paprika.

ADAPTABLE FISH STEW

Adapts to your area and the season. Unlike most fish dishes, it ages well and is even better the third day.

3 medium zucchini

4 to 5 stalks celery

1 pound green beans

1 green pepper, seeded

2 medium onions

1 garlic clove, crushed

3 tablespoons vegetable oil

½ teaspoon lemon pepper

1 teaspoon basil

½ teaspoon Lawry's seasoned salt

1 (10-ounce) can Snap-E-Tom

2 (5½-ounce) cans Mott's Clamato

1 (24-ounce) can V-8

2 (24-ounce) cans tomatoes

1 pound firm white fish (red snapper, ling cod, scrod, etc.)

1 cup dry sherry

12 fresh clams or large shrimp

Makes 5 quarts.

Chop fresh vegetables into bite-size pieces. Toss in hot oil with crushed garlic. Add seasonings, then juices and tomatoes; bring to a boil. Reduce heat and simmer 15 minutes. Add the white fish which has been cut in generous bite-size pieces; add sherry. Simmer a few minutes until fish is done (opaque).

Remove from heat and let the stew sit and soak overnight in refrigerator.

When ready to serve, add clams or shrimp and bring just to a boil. Adjust seasonings and serve immediately.

Featured

Players

ENTRÉES

ROAST BEEF TENDERLOIN WITH BORDELAISE SAUCE

Best Bordelaise Sauce ever.

¼ cup flour

½ cup butter, softened

½ teaspoon salt

1 whole beef tenderloin (4 to 7 pounds), tied

Serves 8 to 10.

Make a paste by gradually adding flour to softened butter; add salt.

Arrange tenderloin in baking pan and spread with the paste (paste helps retain juices, making meat moist and delicious). Bake at 550° for 30 to 45 minutes, depending on size and degree of doneness you desire.

Cut tenderloin into 1-inch slices; arrange on heated platter. Spoon some Bordelaise Sauce over slices and pass remaining sauce.

BORDELAISE SAUCE

2 tablespoons butter

1 shallot, minced

1 onion slice

2 carrot slices

1 tablespoon parsley, chopped

1 whole clove

6 whole black peppercorns

½ bay leaf

2 tablespoons flour

1 (10½-ounce) can beef bouillon, undiluted

¼ teaspoon salt

⅛ teaspoon pepper

¼ cup dry red wine

Makes 1¼ cups.

In skillet, melt butter and sauté shallot, onion, carrot and parsley. Add clove, peppercorns and bay leaf. When onion is golden and tender, add flour. Cook over low heat until flour is lightly brown, stirring constantly. Add bouillon; stir over heat about 10 minutes until thick; strain. Add salt and pepper and red wine. Refrigerate. Sauce may be made several days in advance.

About 20 minutes before serving, reheat, covered, in double boiler. If sauce is too thick, thin with a little wine.

PERFECT BEEF ROAST

For a tender and juicy roast, try either of these two versions.

Beef roast

Seasonings to taste

For a roast weighing less than 10 pounds, preheat oven to 375°. Have meat at room temperature. Place roast on rack in shallow pan. Roast 1 hour at 375°. Turn oven off; do not open door. For medium rare, leave roast in oven 3 to 3¼ hours. Turn oven to 300° for 20 minutes before removing from oven. Let stand 15 minutes before carving.

For a 10 to 12 pound roast, start it at 375° in late morning. Roast for 1½ hours, turn off oven and leave all day without opening door. One to two hours before serving, turn oven on to 275°; a roast cooked for one hour will be medium rare. Let stand 15 minutes before carving.

NEWMAN'S OWN MARINATED STEAK

½ cup Newman's Own Olive Oil and Vinegar Dressing

2 cloves garlic, crushed

1 large onion, cut up

Salt and pepper

1 large sirloin steak, about 1½ inches thick

Serves 4.

Combine Newman's Own, garlic, onion, dash of salt and pepper in a shallow glass dish. Add steak; turn to coat with marinade. Refrigerate several hours, turning steak occasionally.

Just before serving preheat broiler or grill. Drain steak; broil or grill. Slice and serve.

Paul Newman

One of Hollywood's favorite actors. A well-known chef who markets his own line of food products; profits are donated to charities.

SAUTÉED STEAK WITH SHALLOT SAUCE

Sauce pleasingly enhances beef flavor.

4 tenderloin or top loin steaks or 4 lean
   ground round patties

Salt and pepper to taste

½ teaspoon vegetable oil

2 tablespoons butter

½ cup shallots, finely sliced

2 tablespoons tarragon wine vinegar

½ teaspoon dried tarragon

2 tablespoons parsley, finely chopped

Serves 4.

Season steaks or patties on both sides with salt and pepper. Heat oil in heavy skillet and sauté meat on both sides just short of desired doneness (meat will continue to cook slightly from its own heat). Remove to heated platter and keep warm while preparing sauce. Pour off any fat in pan.

Add butter and shallots to skillet and sauté until tender. Add vinegar and tarragon; heat and pour over steaks. Sprinkle with parsley. Serve immediately.

FLANK STEAK MARINADE

A family favorite that is often requested.

¼ cup salad oil

¼ cup dry vermouth

¼ cup soy sauce

1 to 2 teaspoons prepared mustard

1 clove minced garlic (optional)

½ teaspoon dry mustard

¼ teaspoon pepper

¼ teaspoon salt

2 teaspoons Worcestershire sauce

Flank steak

Serves 4 to 6.

Combine all ingredients except meat; blend 1 to 2 minutes on medium speed of blender. Pour over flank steak and marinate overnight; turn the next morning.

Grill to desired doneness and slice meat on the diagonal.

JALAPEÑO FLANK STEAK

½ cup canned tomato sauce

½ cup dry red wine

½ teaspoon chili powder

Flank steak (2 to 3 pounds)

2 tablespoons butter

½ teaspoon cumin

1 (8-ounce) package Kraft Jalapeño cheese

Serves 4 to 6.

Combine first 3 ingredients; marinate steak in mixture at least 3 hours or overnight.

In a small saucepan, combine butter, cumin and cheese. Cook over low heat just until cheese melts.

Grill steak over coals or broil 6 minutes on first side and 4 minutes on second side. Spread cheese on top of steak last two minutes or until melted.

Slice thinly and serve immediately.

VEAL MEDALLIONS ARGENTEUIL

2 pounds veal medallions

Flour

½ cup butter (1 cube)

2 shallots, finely chopped

¾ cup dry white wine

2 cups whipping cream

Salt and pepper to taste

Juice of 1 lemon

Serves 4.

Dry medallions with paper towels. Lightly flour them and sauté in butter with shallots. Add white wine; cook gently for 5 minutes. Remove medallions from pan and keep warm.

Add cream to the wine; add salt and pepper. Reduce to half. Add lemon juice. Stir a few seconds and pour over medallions. If you prefer more sauce, add more cream. Serve with fresh asparagus and potatoes sautéed French style.

James and Ginette DePreist

James is the beloved maestro of the Oregon Symphony Orchestra; Ginette is a former star of radio in Quebec.

SPRINGTIME VEAL STEW

The most eye appealing stew ever.

4 carrots, cut in 2-inch pieces

3 celery stalks, cut in large pieces

¼ cup olive oil

1 clove garlic, minced

6 small red potatoes

1 green pepper, cut in large pieces

1 red pepper, cut in large pieces

1 white onion, coarsely chopped

1 pound veal stew meat

Flour

½ cup dry white wine, divided

½ to 1 tablespoon rosemary

1 tablespoon basil

Salt and pepper

1 tablespoon Dijon mustard

Serves 4.

In ovenproof pan, sauté carrots and celery in olive oil and garlic for 5 minutes; remove from pan. Sauté potatoes for 5 minutes; remove. Sauté peppers and onions 2 minutes; remove.

Toss veal in flour and brown in same pan. Add ¼ cup white wine. Place vegetables in pan; add seasonings.

Cook covered, 45 minutes at 325°. Uncover and add remaining ¼ cup white wine and the Dijon mustard; stir. Cook for another 15 minutes.

CHILLED VEAL LOAF

Elegant choice for a hot summer day.

2 cups ground veal

1 cup cooked ham, chopped or ground

2 cups bread crumbs, moistened with 1 cup hot water

1½ cups grated Cheddar cheese

1 teaspoon celery salt

1 cup cooked macaroni

3 eggs

1 medium onion, chopped fine

Salt and pepper plus any seasoning you prefer

Milk (optional)

Bacon strips (optional)

Currant jelly

Serves 6 to 8.

Preheat oven to 350°.

Combine all ingredients. Press firmly into loaf pan. Bake for 1 hour. During baking, baste with milk or cover with bacon strips before baking.

Chill before slicing; serve with currant jelly. This should be served very cold.

VENISON STEAK WITH CRACKED PEPPER

Venison steak covered with freshly cracked pepper and a light brandy sauce is truly delicious. The secret of keeping the meat juicy is to sear it quickly in order to seal it. A horseradish and sour cream sauce is a good accompaniment.

2 pounds venison round steak

¼ cup brandy

2 tablespoons butter or safflower oil

Salt

Freshly cracked pepper

Chopped fresh parsley, for garnish

Serves 4.

Pat the meat dry; rub it with butter or oil and a generous coating of freshly cracked pepper. Let it sit at room temperature for at least an hour.

Heat a large skillet over moderately high heat and add the oil. Place the meat in the pan and cook for about 2 minutes, or until the juices begin accumulating on the top. Turn and cook for another 2 minutes. Do not turn again. Transfer the meat to a warm platter.

Scrape the bottom of the pan to collect all of the cooking juices and add the brandy. Cook over high heat 1 to 2 minutes, then add the salt and more pepper, if necessary. Pour over the meat.

Garnish the steak with chopped parsley and serve immediately.

Jane Hibler

Jane Hibler

Cookbook author and food columnist for The Oregonian.

CAST PARTY MEATBALLS

1 egg, slightly beaten

1 pound lean ground beef

1 tablespoon instant minced onion

¼ teaspoon dry mustard

¼ teaspoon ground ginger

¼ cup fine dry bread or cracker crumbs

¼ to ½ teaspoon salt

⅛ teaspoon pepper

2 tablespoons salad oil for browning

3 to 4 tablespoons soy sauce

¼ cup water

2 tablespoons sugar

¼ teaspoon garlic powder or 1 clove fresh garlic, crushed

2 slices fresh ginger root

Makes 35 to 40.

Combine first 8 ingredients and mix thoroughly. Shape into small meatballs about ¾ inch in diameter. Roll in flour on sheet of waxed paper, gently tapping off excess. Brown in oil, turning meatballs on all sides to brown evenly. Drain off any accumulated fat.

Combine remaining ingredients and pour over meatballs. Cover and cook over low heat for about 20 minutes. You may need to add water or wine as the meatballs simmer. Discard ginger root slices. When cooked, the meatballs should be brown and glazed, moistened with sauce but not floating in it.

Serve hot. If using as an hors d'oeuvre, serve speared on toothpicks or skewers, or in a chafing dish with toothpicks available.

Milli Hoelscher

Milli Hoelscher

Lake Oswego Community Theater director and producer, and high school drama teacher.

GERMAN MEAT BALLS

Testers who have lived in Germany declared these authentic and good.

1 cup raw potato, coarsely grated

1 pound lean ground beef

Grind of black pepper

1 tablespoon chopped parsley

1 teaspoon seasoned salt

1 teaspoon onion, minced

1 teaspoon lemon peel, grated

1 egg, slightly beaten

3 teaspoons cornstarch, divided

2½ cups beef bouillon

½ teaspoon caraway seeds

1 tablespoon cold water

Serves 4 to 6.

Mix first 8 ingredients. Form into 1½-inch balls and roll in 2 teaspoons cornstarch.

Put bouillon in deep pot with tight cover. Bring to a boil and drop meatballs in one at a time. Cover and simmer for 30 minutes. Remove meat balls with slotted spoon and keep hot.

Add a little freshly ground black pepper and the caraway seeds to stock in which meatballs were cooked. Simmer, uncovered, for 10 minutes. Mix remaining teaspoon cornstarch with the cold water and stir into stock. Cook, stirring until sauce has thickened. Combine with meatballs and serve.

STUFFED ZUCCHINI

12 to 14 small zucchini, cut in half, lengthwise

6 tablespoons olive oil

3 cloves garlic, finely chopped

⅔ cup bread crumbs or croutons

12 black olives, chopped

1 small tomato, seeded and chopped

2 tablespoons chopped parsley

¼ to ½ pound lean ground beef, lightly sautéed with all grease strained off

Salt and pepper

Additional bread crumbs

Freshly grated Parmesan cheese

Serves 6.

Scoop out and discard seeds and small amount of flesh from zucchini. Quickly sauté halves in olive oil, then parboil 5 to 10 minutes; cool.

Sauté garlic and crumbs in olive oil for 2 minutes. Add olives, tomato, parsley, beef and seasonings. Mix and stuff into zucchini halves. Sprinkle with bread crumbs and Parmesan cheese.

Arrange in baking dish and bake at 375° for 20 minutes.

If using large summer zucchini, do not sauté in oil. Bake longer. Test with fork for doneness.

BABOOTIE

A South African native dish with a taste as distinctive as its name, and oh, so good.

2 pounds ground beef

2 onions, grated or chopped

2 cloves garlic, chopped

1 (16-ounce) can stewed tomatoes, chopped in small pieces

1½ tablespoons sugar

2 tablespoons curry powder

2 tablespoons vinegar

1 to 2 teaspoons salt

2 firm bananas, sliced

2 apples, peeled and diced

½ cup raisins (optional)

¼ cup slivered almonds

Tomato paste as needed to thicken

Serves 4 to 6.

Brown beef and onions in large skillet; drain off excess fat. Add all other ingredients. Simmer gently, stirring frequently, for 30 minutes.

Serve over rice.

CALIFORNIA CASSEROLE

1½ pounds lean ground beef, browned

1 clove garlic, chopped

1 teaspoon salt

½ teaspoon pepper

1 teaspoon sugar

1 (6-ounce) can tomato paste

3 (8-ounce) cans tomato sauce

4 ounces cream cheese

1 cup sour cream

1 bunch green onions, chopped

½ cup pitted sliced olives, chopped

1 (8-ounce) package wide noodles

1 tablespoon butter

1 cup Cheddar cheese, grated

Serves 6 or more.

Combine meat, garlic, salt, pepper, sugar, tomato paste and tomato sauce. Cook uncovered 15 to 20 minutes, stir well.

Mix cream cheese, sour cream, chopped onions and olives.

Cook noodles in salt water; drain; toss with butter.

Spoon about 1 cup meat sauce into a 2-quart casserole ; spread noodles on top. Cover noodles with rest of meat sauce, then cream cheese and onion mixture. Top with Cheddar cheese. Cook at 350° for 30 minutes or until bubbly.

John Raitt

John Raitt

Golden voiced star of screen and stage, well remembered for The Pajama Game.

JOHNNY MARZETTI

2 tablespoons butter

2 large onions, diced

1½ pounds ground beef

1 teaspoon salt

¼ teaspoon pepper

1 (6-ounce) can tomato paste

8 ounces mushrooms, sliced

1½ cups water

1 cup celery, diced

1 teaspoon vinegar

½ pound sharp cheese, grated

1 green pepper, diced (optional)

8 ounces broad noodles

¼ to ½ cup buttered bread crumbs

Serves 6 to 8.

Melt butter in large skillet. Add onions and cook until limp. Add ground beef, salt and pepper; brown well. Add remaining ingredients except noodles and bread crumbs; simmer 15 minutes to make a rich sauce.

Meanwhile, cook noodles in boiling salted water until just tender; drain. Mix with sauce in 1½-quart casserole. Cover with buttered bread crumbs.

Bake uncovered at 350° for 1 hour. Freezes well.

MOUSSAKA À LA GRECQUE

3 medium eggplants

1 cup butter, a few tablespoons at a time

3 large onions, chopped

2 pounds ground beef

3 tablespoons tomato paste

½ cup red wine

½ cup chopped parsley

¼ teaspoon cinnamon

Salt and pepper to taste

8 tablespoons butter

6 tablespoons flour

1 quart milk

4 eggs, beaten slightly

Nutmeg

2 cups Ricotta cheese

1 cup fine bread crumbs

1 cup Parmesan cheese, grated

Serves 8.

Peel eggplant and cut in slices about ½-inch thick. Brown in butter, then remove and set aside. Heat more butter in same pan and cook onions until brown. Add meat; cook 10 minutes. Combine tomato paste, wine, parsley, cinnamon, salt and pepper. Stir into meat and simmer slowly, stirring until liquid is absorbed.

Make white sauce by melting 8 tablespoons butter in saucepan over medium high heat. Add flour and stir constantly to be sure all flour taste has disappeared. Slowly add boiling milk and stir until thickened. Remove from heat; cool slightly. Stir in eggs, nutmeg, and ricotta.

Grease an 11 x 16-inch pan; sprinkle bottom lightly with bread crumbs. Alternate layers of eggplant, meat sauce, white sauce, Parmesan cheese and bread crumbs, ending with white sauce.

Bake at 375° for 1 hour. May be baked in advance and reheated.

DEEP DISH LASAGNA

This beats all other lasagnas.

2 strips bacon

1 pound ground beef

2 cloves garlic, crushed

2 teaspoons olive oil

1 (6-ounce) can tomato paste

1 (8-ounce) can tomato sauce

1½ teaspoons salt

½ teaspoon ground pepper

½ teaspoon cayenne

½ teaspoon oregano

1 carrot, diced

3 tablespoons chopped parsley

¼ cup dry red wine

8 ounces whole lasagna noodles

½ pound Mozzarella cheese, grated

½ pound Romano cheese, grated

¾ pound Ricotta cheese

Serves 6.

Brown bacon until crisp; crumble and set aside. Brown beef and garlic in olive oil; drain fat. Add remaining ingredients except noodles and cheeses. Simmer until thick. If sauce becomes too thick, thin with more wine.

Boil noodles in salted water until nearly tender; drain. Reserving a bit of sauce and a bit of Romano for top, spoon a small amount of sauce into the bottom of a deep casserole, then layer noodles, cheeses and sauce, repeating layers and ending with noodles. Top with reserved sauce, crumbled bacon and Romano. Cover with foil and bake at least 30 minutes at 375°, though flavor is improved by longer cooking at 350°. Remove foil for last 15 minutes of baking time. May be baked, refrigerated overnight and reheated before serving.

CURRIED BEEF PITA

1 pound ground beef

1 medium onion, diced

1 garlic clove, mashed

1 to 2 teaspoons curry powder

1 medium zucchini, diced

½ cup water

1 teaspoon salt

½ teaspoon sugar

¼ teaspoon pepper

1 medium tomato, diced

¾ to 1 cup sour cream

4 pita or Middle East bread rounds

Serves 4.

In 10-inch skillet over medium high heat, cook ground beef, onion, garlic and curry powder until meat is browned and onion tender, about 10 minutes, stirring frequently. Drain any fat or liquid.

Add zucchini, water, salt, sugar and pepper; heat to boiling. Reduce heat to low; cover and simmer 15 minutes, stirring occasionally.

Stir in tomato; heat through.

Stir in sour cream. Mix well and heat through.

Cut each pita bread in half to make pockets. Heat in 350° oven about 5 minutes. Fill each pocket with meat mixture. Serve immediately.

OLD SETTLER BEEF AND BEANS

½ pound bacon, diced

1 pound ground beef

1 large onion, chopped

¼ cup barbecue sauce

¼ cup catsup

⅓ cup granulated sugar

⅓ cup brown sugar

1 teaspoon salt

1 tablespoon chili powder

1 tablespoon prepared mustard

2 tablespoons molasses

1 (15-ounce) can pork and beans

1 (15-ounce) can butter beans

1 (15-ounce) can kidney beans

1 (15-ounce) can chili beans

Serves 6 to 8.

Brown bacon, ground beef and onion. Pour off excess fat.

Mix together next 8 ingredients and add to meat mixture. Add canned beans including all juice from pork and beans and chili beans, plus about half of the juice from the butter and kidney beans. Pour into large casserole.

Bake at 350° for 1 hour.

This recipe can be doubled or tripled. Cooking time varies depending on depth of casserole.

LAMB CROWN ROAST WITH CARROT STUFFING

An Easter favorite.

3½ to 4 pound lamb crown roast, well trimmed

Salt

Pepper

½ cup celery, chopped

½ cup onion, finely chopped

2 tablespoons butter

1 beef bouillon cube

1½ cups hot water

4 cups dry bread cubes, unseasoned

1 medium carrot,grated

1 teaspoon salt

⅛ teaspoon pepper

⅛ teaspoon marjoram

1 egg, well beaten

Serves 6 to 7.

Season roast; place on rack rib ends down. Roast in 325° oven for 1½ hours.

To prepare stuffing, sauté celery and onion in butter. Dissolve bouillon in water. Combine with all remaining ingredients; mix well.

Remove roast from oven and turn so rib ends are up; stuff. Roast 1 to 1½ hours more or until meat thermometer registers 165° or desired doneness.

DOUBLE COATED RACK OF LAMB

Lamb rack should be served on the rare side; be careful not to overcook.

2 lamb racks, well trimmed

4 tablespoons Dijon mustard

1½ tablespoons soy sauce

1 teaspoon thyme

¼ teaspoon ground ginger

3 tablespoons olive oil

¾ cup bread crumbs

5 tablespoons butter

¼ cup minced fresh parsley

½ teaspoon thyme

Salt and pepper to taste

Serves 6.

Preheat oven to 475°.

To make mustard coating, mix mustard with soy sauce, thyme and ginger; whisk in olive oil 1 tablespoon at a time. Spread over lamb 2 hours before roasting; leave at room temperature.

To make parsley coating, melt butter in small skillet, add remaining ingredients and cook 2 to 3 minutes, stirring constantly.

Roast with mustard coating 15 minutes. Remove from oven and pat on parsley coating. Reduce heat to 450°; return lamb to oven and roast until meat thermometer reads 135° to 140°. Let sit 5 minutes; carve into chops. Serve immediately.

LEG OF LAMB WITH PESTO STUFFING

Prepared pesto may be substituted if fresh basil is not available.

4 to 5 pound leg of lamb, boned

1 cup fresh basil, tightly packed

3 tablespoons walnuts

2 cloves garlic, minced

½ cup olive oil

½ teaspoon salt

Serves 6 to 8.

Preheat oven to 325°. Trim all fat from meat.

Place remaining ingredients in blender or food processor and blend well. Spread this sauce in cavity of roast; roll up and tie. Season. Roast until medium rare, about 140° on meat thermometer. Leave at room temperature for 15 minutes before serving.

PEPPERED BARBECUED LEG OF LAMB

Try wild rice with this picquant lamb recipe.

5 pound leg of lamb

2 cups dry red wine

2 teaspoons salt

2 teaspoons poultry seasoning

3 cloves garlic, mashed

Coarsely ground pepper, enough to coat

Serves 8.

Have lamb leg boned and butterflied so it lays flat.

Mix remaining ingredients except pepper; marinate lamb for 24 hours in refrigerator. Drain, coat well with pepper.

Cook over medium hot coals for 45 minutes. Meat should be light pink when cut diagonally in ¼ inch slices.

LAMB SHANKS WITH CARAWAY SAUCE

A hearty and wholesome winter entrée.

4 lamb shanks

2 cloves garlic, pressed

2 medium onions, chopped

¼ cup chopped fresh parsley

1 teaspoon salt

1 tablespoon paprika

2 tablespoons lemon juice

2 large tomatoes, peeled and sliced

1 cup dry white wine

1 teaspoon caraway seeds

1 cup plain yogurt or sour cream

1 tablespoon flour

Serves 4.

Brown lamb shanks and place in oven casserole. Blend garlic, onions, parsley, salt, paprika and lemon juice; spread over shanks. Place sliced tomatoes on top and pour wine over all. Cover and bake at 400° for 1½ to 2 hours or until tender.

Drain pan juices into small pan. Add caraway seeds and boil until reduced to ¾ cup. Blend yogurt and flour until smooth, then stir into pan juices. Cook 2 minutes, then add to casserole.

Serve sauce with lamb on a bed of rice.

LAMB SHANKS JARDINIÈRE

This makes an especially tasty gravy to serve over rice or mashed potatoes.

4 meaty lamb shanks, cut in half

1 lemon

½ teaspoon garlic powder, or more

1 cup flour

2 teaspoons salt

½ teaspoon pepper

½ cup salad oil

1 (10½-ounce) can condensed beef consommé, undiluted

1 cup water

½ cup dry vermouth

1 medium yellow onion, chopped

4 carrots, peeled and cut in chunks

4 stalks celery, cut in chunks

Serves 4.

Rub lamb with cut lemon and sprinkle with garlic powder; let stand 10 minutes. Mix flour, salt and pepper in bag; shake shanks one at a time to coat with flour; save flour.

Brown shanks in hot oil in heavy skillet. Remove meat from pan. Add 2 tablespoons reserved seasoned flour to pan drippings. Using a wire whip, stir and brown flour. Add consommé, water and vermouth; stir and cook until slightly thickened. Add onion.

Place shanks in one layer in large baking dish; pour consommé mix over them. Refrigerate.

When ready to bake, place in 350° oven, uncovered, for 1½ hours. Turn shanks; add carrots and celery and continue to bake 1 hour. Gravy is delicious over mashed potatoes.

ROAST PORK PROVENÇAL

The olive oil and rosemary recall flavors of the south of France.

3 to 4 pound pork roast

3 garlic cloves, peeled

Garlic salt

Pepper

1½ teaspoons rosemary, crushed

3 tablespoons olive oil

Serves 4 to 6.

Preheat oven to 400°. Make 3 slashes in roast; stuff a garlic clove in each. Rub with garlic salt, pepper and rosemary. Drizzle olive oil over top of roast.

Place in 400° oven; immediately reduce heat to 325°; roast until meat thermometer registers 170° or desired temperature.

ROAST PORK AND SAUERKRAUT

5 to 6 pound pork loin roast, well-trimmed

¾ teaspoon salt

¼ teaspoon pepper

2 pounds canned sauerkraut, drained

1 large yellow onion, chopped

1 garlic clove, sliced

1 (6-ounce) can frozen apple juice concentrate, thawed

Serves 6 to 8.

Preheat oven to 500°. Season roast with salt and pepper; place on rack in roasting pan; brown in hot oven 10 minutes. Remove from oven; pour off accumulated fat. Reduce oven heat to 300°. Remove rack from roasting pan.

Heat sauerkraut and onion in a saucepan. Spoon over roast; place garlic cloves on top; add apple juice concentrate. Cover tightly and bake 3½ hours or until tender.

Cut pork in thick slices and serve with sauerkraut.

CHINESE BARBECUED PORK

2 pounds lean, boneless pork (loin or butt)

Marinade:

2 green onions or shallots, minced

2 teaspoons powdered ginger or 1 teaspoon
grated fresh ginger

2 tablespoons honey

1 clove garlic, crushed

¼ teaspoon Chinese fivespice seasoning

1 teaspoon salt

1 tablespoon Hoisin sauce

⅓ cup sugar

Basting sauce:

2 teaspoons sesame oil

1 tablespoon sugar

1 tablespoon soy sauce

1½ teaspoons hot water

Serves 4 to 6.

Cut pork into strips 6 inches long and 1 inch thick. Combine marinade ingredients; pour over pork and marinate, refrigerate at least 3 hours but not more than 6.

Preheat oven to 450°. Remove pork strips from marinade and place on rack of broiler pan. Add basting sauce to remaining marinade. Bake pork on second rack of oven about 25 minutes, turning and basting every 10 minutes. (To baste, remove pork strips from rack, dip in sauce, then return to rack.)

Note: If you double this recipe, do not double sugar; use ½ cup.

SZECHUAN PORK CHOPS

2 large cloves garlic, minced

2 green onions, minced

1 teaspoon fresh ginger, minced

2 tablespoons soy sauce

1 tablespoon sesame oil

2½ teaspoons lemon juice

1 teaspoon sugar

½ teaspoon Chinese hot chili oil

2 teaspoons Chinese chili paste

4 pork chops, 1-inch thick

Serves 4.

Combine all ingredients except chops. Pour over chops and refrigerate overnight in a non-metallic dish or zip-lock bag.

Grill over hot coals or broil.

PIQUANT PORK CHOPS

6 loin pork chops

3 tablespoons margarine

½ cup onions, minced

1 tablespoon flour

Few grains pepper

¾ cup condensed chicken broth, undiluted

½ cup Rhine wine

2 tablespoons wine vinegar

¼ cup sweet gherkins, sliced

1 tablespoon sherry

Serves 6.

Brown chops slowly on both sides in margarine about 30 minutes. Add onions; cook until golden brown. Remove chops. Sprinkle flour and pepper into skillet; stir until brown. Add broth gradually, stirring constantly. Add Rhine wine, vinegar and gherkins; simmer one minute. Return chops to skillet; simmer 10 minutes, covered. Stir in sherry just before serving.

PORK CHOPS DIJON

2 to 4 pork chops, well trimmed

1 large onion, thinly sliced

Dijon mustard

Salt

Pepper

Serves 2 to 4.

Gently brown chops on one side; turn and spread mustard generously over each. Top each with slice of onion. Grind fresh pepper over all; salt lightly. Cover and cook gently 20 minutes or more, depending on thickness of chops; thinly sliced chops work best.

SPAGHETTI CON ZUCCHINI E SALSICCIA

1 pound fresh mushrooms, thinly sliced

½ cup butter (I cube)

1½ pounds mild Italian sausage, cut very small

½ cup dry white wine

6 chicken bouillon cubes or 6 teaspoons instant chicken bouillon

1½ pounds zucchini, cut in small pieces

½ cup green onion tops, chopped

8 tomatoes, peeled and chopped

1 pound thin spaghetti, broken in half

Serves 8.

In Dutch oven or very large frying pan, sauté mushrooms in melted butter; remove from pan; add sausage and brown. Add wine and bouillon; stir until bouillon dissolves. Add zucchini, onions, and tomatoes. Cook over medium heat, uncovered, until zucchini is barely tender and sausage is done, about 20 minutes.

Meanwhile, cook spagetti according to package directions until tender but firm to the bite. Drain well in colander; combine with sauce.

This may be made in advance and reheated, covered, though some of the crispness of the zucchini may be lost.

OUR FAVORITE HAM

Half ham, shank end, bone-in

Water to cover

1 tablespoon whole cloves

3 cloves garlic

1 cup sugar

1 cup vinegar

1 cup brown sugar

3 tablespoons prepared mustard

Whole cloves

Allow ¼ pound per serving.

In large stockpot or canning kettle, bring water to boil. Add cloves, garlic, sugar, and vinegar; stir to dissolve sugar. Plunge ham into the liquid; if necessary, add enough boiling water to cover. Immediately remove from heat and allow to cool in liquid at least 4 hours.

Remove ham from broth; skin and trim some of the fat. Place on rack in roasting pan; cover loosely with foil tent and bake at 300° for 1½ hours.

Remove foil; score fat. Combine brown sugar and mustard, pat on ham; decorate with cloves. Return to oven; bake at 350° for at least another hour.

This process produces a moist, fine-textured ham of excellent flavor.

HAM AND CAULIFLOWER AU GRATIN

1 medium head cauliflower

2 tablespoons butter or margarine

2 tablespoons flour

1 cup milk

4 ounces sharp Cheddar cheese, grated

½ cup sour cream

2 cups cooked ham, chopped

4 ounces mushrooms, sliced

1 cup bread crumbs

1 tablespoon butter or margarine, melted

Serves 4.

Break cauliflower into buds. Cook, covered, until barely tender; drain and set aside.

Melt butter in saucepan; stir in flour. Add milk and cook, stirring constantly, until thick; remove from heat. Add cheese; stir until melted. Add sour cream, cauliflower, ham and mushrooms. Pour into greased casserole. Combine bread crumbs and melted butter; sprinkle on top. Bake at 350°, uncovered, until hot and bubbling, about 25 minutes.

CHRISTINE'S CALZONE

By special request and "guaranteed delicious" by its contributor.

Dough:

1 package active dry yeast

1 cup warm (110°) water

½ teaspoon salt

2 teaspoons olive or salad oil

2½ to 3 cups flour

Sausage Filling:

3 mild Italian sausages (about 10 ounces)

1 small onion, sliced

1 clove garlic, minced

¼ pound mushrooms, sliced

1 small green pepper, sliced

1 small carrot, thinly sliced

1 (8-ounce) can tomato sauce

1 (2¼-ounce) can sliced olives, drained

1 teaspoon dry basil

½ teaspoon oregano

½ teaspoon sugar

¼ teaspoon crushed red pepper

2 cups Mozzarella cheese, grated

½ cup Parmesan cheese, grated

Salt and pepper

Serves 4.

Dissolve yeast in water; stir in salt and oil. Gradually mix in enough flour to make a soft dough. Turn onto well-floured board; knead until smooth and not sticky, adding more flour as needed. Place in greased bowl; turn dough to grease top. Cover and let rise in warm place until double in bulk, about an hour.

Slice sausages and brown in a large frying pan over medium heat. Add onion, garlic, mushrooms, green pepper and carrot; cook, stirring, until vegetables are tender. Add remaining filling ingredients except cheeses. Simmer, uncovered, about 5 minutes; cool.

When ready to assemble add cheeses to filling and salt and pepper to taste. Stir down dough and knead lightly to break up bubbles. Divide into 4 portions. Shape each portion into a round ball and roll into a 8½-inch circle. Brush surface of each lightly with oil. Spread divided portion of filling on one half of each circle. Fold plain half over filling ; press edges together. Roll ½ inch edge up and over; seal and crimp. Grease baking sheets; dust with cornmeal. Using a wide spatula, transfer turnovers to baking sheets. Prick tops with fork; brush with oil. Bake at 475° until well-browned, 15 to 20 minutes. Best when fresh, but leftovers may be reheated in a 350° oven 25 to 30 minutes.

Vegetable Filling Variation: Follow recipe for sausage filling, omitting sausage and cooking vegetables in 2 to 3 tablespoons oil. Increase mushrooms to ½ pound, oregano to 1 teaspoon, Mozzarella to 2½ cups and Parmesan to ¾ cup. Add ½ teaspoon fennel seed if desired.

CHICKEN BREASTS IN PASTRY

An attractive and elegant recipe that may be prepared ahead of time.

½ cup butter(1 cube) plus 2 tablespoons

4 ounces cream cheese

1 cup flour

2 whole chicken breasts, boned, skinned and halved

Salt and pepper

1 egg, lightly beaten

1 tablespoon water

Dill Sauce:

4 tablespoons butter

2 tablespoons flour

1 cup chicken broth

Salt and pepper to taste

1 tablespoon fresh dill, or 1½ teaspoons dried dill weed

Serves 4.

Soften ½ cup butter and cream cheese; blend together. Add flour; mix with a fork until pastry leaves sides of bowl. Divide into four equal parts; wrap each separately in waxed paper. Chill at least 1 hour.

Sauté chicken breasts in 2 tablespoons butter 2 to 3 minutes on each side. Sprinkle with salt and pepper.

Preheat oven to 425°. Roll each portion of pastry thinly on lightly floured board. Place half a chicken breast on each piece of pastry. Fold pastry over chicken, pinching to seal. Place seam side down on lightly greased baking sheet. Cut small leaf shapes out of leftover pastry and arrange on tops of chicken bundles. Combine beaten egg with water and brush on top of each pastry; prick several places with a fork. Bake until crust is well browned, about 20 minutes. Serve with dill sauce.

To make sauce, melt butter, add flour and stir 2 minutes; add chicken stock. Cook over medium heat, stirring constantly, until thickened. Season with salt, pepper, and dill.

Baja California Chicken

8 boned chicken breasts
Seasoning salt and pepper, to taste
2 cloves garlic, crushed

4 tablespoons olive oil
4 tablespoons tarragon vinegar
⅔ cup dry sherry

Sprinkle chicken with seasoning salt and pepper. Crush garlic into oil and vinegar in a skillet. Saute chicken pieces until golden brown, turning frequently. Remove; place in a baking dish. Pour sherry over pieces and place in 350 degree oven for 10 minutes.

Yield: 8 servings.

With best wishes, *Nancy Reagan*

CHICKEN MELANIE

For garlic lovers.

2 whole chicken breasts, boned, skinned and halved

3 eggs, beaten

2 cups fresh bread crumbs

4 tablespoons butter

Sauce:

⅓ cup butter

¼ cup fresh lemon juice

¼ cup dry white wine

1 teaspoon dried tarragon

2 to 3 cloves fresh garlic, minced

¼ cup chopped fresh parsley

Serves 4.

Between two sheets of waxed paper, pound chicken until fairly thin. Dip chicken pieces in beaten egg, then in crumbs, coating generously. Melt 2 tablespoons butter in a large skillet over medium heat. Fry chicken until lightly browned on each side, adding remaining 2 tablespoons butter as needed. Cook until chicken loses its translucency, taking care not to overcook.

Combine first four sauce ingredients in a small saucepan and simmer about 4 minutes. Add garlic and parsley; continue simmering another 4 minutes.

Transfer chicken to a warmed serving platter and pour a generous amount of sauce over each piece. Serve immediately with French bread to soak up extra sauce.

HOT CHICKEN SALAD

Makes a wonderful cold salad too, using all the ingredients except cheese and chips; just mix and chill.

2 cups cooked chicken breasts, diced

1½ cups celery, thinly sliced

½ cup slivered almonds, toasted

1 cup mayonnaise

1 tablespoon onion, grated

2 tablespoons lemon juice

Topping:

1 cup Cheddar cheese, grated

1 cup potato chips, finely crushed

Serves 6.

Combine first six ingredients in saucepan. Place over low heat; warm gently. If overheated, mixture will separate.

Turn into greased casserole. Sprinkle with cheese and potato chips. Place in 450° oven for 10 minutes or until lightly browned.

Serve in lettuce cups.

CHICKEN MAZZANTI

A tantalizing combination.

2 whole chicken breasts, boned, skinned and halved

1 ounce Monterey Jack cheese

4 sprigs fresh sage, or ½ teaspoon dried

2 eggs

1 tablespoon grated Parmesan cheese

1 tablespoon instant chicken bouillon granules

1 teaspoon parsley, snipped

Dash pepper

3 tablespoons flour

Lime slices

Parsley sprigs

Serves 4.

On thickest side, cut a pocket in each piece of chicken. Cut cheese into 4 slices about 1 x 3 inches. Insert a slice of cheese and a sprig of sage into each pocket.

Beat together eggs, Parmesan, bouillon, parsley and pepper. Coat breasts with flour and dip into egg mixture. Brown in hot oil 2 to 3 minutes on each side. Place in small baking pan; bake at 375° for 8 to 10 minutes, or until coating just begins to brown.

Serve with lime slices and parsley sprigs.

CHICKEN MUSHROOM KABOBS

A delicious entrée for a summer barbeque.

2 whole chicken breasts, skinned and boned

10 large mushrooms

¼ cup soy sauce

¼ cup cider vinegar

2 tablespoons honey

2 tablespoons salad oil

2 small green onions, minced

1 (8-ounce) can sliced pineapple, drained

8 ounces lean bacon

Serves 4.

Cut each chicken breast into 5 or 6 chunks. Cut mushrooms in half. In a large bowl, combine soy sauce, vinegar, honey, salad oil and onion. Add chicken and mushrooms; marinate for at least 1½ hours.

Cut each slice of pineapple and each slice of bacon into 3 pieces. Wrap each piece of chicken and a mushroom half with a piece of bacon. Thread on skewers with pineapple pieces between. Baste with marinade.

Cook on grill or under broiler for 15-20 minutes or until bacon is crisp, turning as needed.

POULET PORTUGUESE

Herbs and spices make this unusually good.

3 whole chicken breasts, skinned, boned and halved

Salt and freshly ground pepper

3 tablespoons flour

¼ cup olive oil

3 tablespoons garlic, minced

2 tablespoons paprika

1 cup chicken stock

1 cup pearl onions, parboiled and peeled

½ cup dry vermouth

1 tablespoon basil, crumbled

1 teaspoon thyme, crumbled

1 teaspoon oregano, crumbled

1 cup fresh tomatoes, chopped, seeded and drained

½ cup green onions, chopped

Serves 6.

Season chicken with salt and pepper; dredge in flour, shaking off excess. Heat oil in heavy skillet over medium high heat. Brown chicken well on both sides. Remove from skillet.

Reduce heat to low; add garlic and paprika; stir 3 minutes. Add stock, onions, vermouth and seasonings; bring to a boil. Reduce heat and simmer until onions are tender, about 10 minutes.

Blend in tomatoes. Return chicken to skillet and simmer, covered, until chicken is tender, about 8 minutes. With slotted spoon, transfer chicken to platter, Cover with foil to keep warm. Stir green onions into sauce and cook about 5 minutes. Pour sauce over chicken to serve.

CHICKEN ITALIANO

Great for large dinners; prepare ahead and freeze.

¾ cup bread crumbs

¾ cup Parmesan cheese, grated

½ teaspoon salt

1½ teaspoons garlic powder

½ cup parsley, finely chopped

Dash of pepper

4 tablespoons butter, melted

1 to 2 tablespoons oil

6 to 8 boned chicken breasts or thighs

1 (30-ounce) jar Ragu or Prima Salsa spaghetti sauce

12 ounces Mozzarella cheese, grated

Serves 6 to 8.

Combine first six ingredients for seasoned crumbs. Combine butter and oil in shallow dish or pan. Dip each chicken piece in butter-oil mixture, then roll in seasoned crumbs. Heat remaining butter and oil in skillet; brown chicken lightly.

Spoon a thin layer of spaghetti sauce in the bottom of a 9 x 13-inch baking dish. Arrange chicken pieces on top. Sprinkle with remaining crumb mixture; cover with remaining sauce. Top with grated Mozzarella.

Cover with foil and bake ½ hour at 350°; uncover and bake for another ½ hour.

MEDITERRANEAN MADNESS

One of our contributors saw Johnny Mathis prepare this on TV; when you taste it, you may sing.

8 to 10 boned chicken breasts or thighs (1 to 2 per person)

2 tablespoons butter

2 tablespoons oil

Sauce:

1 (28-ounce) can tomatoes, drained, seeded and chopped

½ cup leeks, chopped

¼ cup chopped parsley

2 bay leaves

2 cloves garlic

1½ teaspoons thyme

1-inch square of orange rind

1 cup dry vermouth

Black olives

Garlic mayonnaise (optional)

Serves 4 to 6.

Heat butter and oil in large skillet; brown chicken lightly. Remove from pan and set aside.

In same skillet, simmer tomatoes, leeks, parsley, bay leaves, garlic, thyme and orange rind until flavors blend, about 10 minutes. Remove bay leaves and orange rind; add vermouth; bring to a boil. Add chicken; reduce heat and simmer 20 minutes, covered.

To serve, surround chicken with sauce; garnish with black olives. If desired, top each piece of chicken with a dollop of mayonnaise to which garlic has been added.

PEANUT CHICKEN

Plan an oriental menu around this recipe.

3 whole chicken breasts, halved, boned and skinned

6 egg whites (1cup)

6 tablespoons cornstarch

2¼ cups cooking oil

½ cup fresh roasted peanuts

¼ cup sliced water chestnuts

¼ cup green peas

¼ cup diced bamboo shoots

¾ cup chicken broth

½ to 1 teaspoon bottled hot pepper sauce

½ teaspoon sugar

½ teaspoon salt

½ teaspoon sesame oil

¼ teaspoon dried hot peppers,crushed (optional)

½ cup cold water

Serves 4 to 6.

Cut chicken into 1 inch slices. Combine egg whites, 4 tablespoons of the cornstarch and 1 tablespoon of the oil; mix well. Pour over chicken and marinate for 1 hour.

In wok or deep skillet, heat 2 cups oil until very hot (365°). With slotted spoon, lift about ¼ of the chicken from marinade and fry in hot oil for 2 minutes. Drain and set aside. Repeat with remaining chicken.

In another wok or pan, heat remaining oil over high heat. Add peanuts and vegetables; stir fry for 2 minutes. Add chicken and broth. Bring to full boil. Add remaining seasonings. Blend remaining 2 tablespoons of cornstarch with cold water and add to boiling mixture. Cook, stirring constantly, until thickened. Serve over rice.

STIR FRY CHICKEN CASHEW

Outstanding; serve with Broccoli Stir Fry and rice for a Far East dinner.

1 egg white, lightly beaten

1 teaspoon fresh ginger, grated

1 tablespoon soy sauce

3 tablespoons cornstarch

2 whole chicken breasts, skinned, boned and cut into bite-size pieces

2 teaspoons soy sauce

2 tablespoons white wine

½ teaspoon vinegar

1 teaspoon salt

1 tablespoon sugar

1 to 2 teaspoons Hoisin sauce

3 to 4 tablespoons oil, divided

1 cup cashews

Serves 4.

Combine first 4 ingredients. Add chicken and marinate in refrigerator at least 20 minutes or several hours.

Combine remaining ingredients except oil and cashews; set aside.

Heat 1 tablespoon oil in wok or heavy skillet. Fry cashews until toasty; remove with slotted spoon and drain.

Add 2 to 3 tablespoons oil; heat. Fry chicken quickly 3 to 4 minutes. Stir in sauce and cashews.

HOISIN CHICKEN

This may be cooked on a grill also; omit foil and brush with marinade.

1 cup soy sauce

½ cup sesame oil

¼ cup Hoisin sauce

¼ cup sugar

¼ cup dry sherry

¼ cup catsup

½ cup scallions or green onions, finely chopped

1 tablespoon powdered ginger

2 cloves garlic, crushed

3 whole chicken breasts, halved

Serves 4 to 6.

Combine all ingredients except chicken. Pour over the chicken and marinate overnight in refrigerator.

Let chicken come to room temperature before cooking. Line baking pan with large sheet of foil. Place chicken on foil; pour marinade over and wrap chicken in foil. Bake at 350° for 50 to 60 minutes.

SESAME CHICKEN

A quickie when you've been out on the town all day.

½ cup butter (1 cube), melted

⅓ cup teriyaki sauce

⅓ cup soy sauce

2 tablespoons sesame oil

3 whole chicken breasts, halved

2 tablespoons sesame seeds

Serves 6.

Melt butter in a 9 x 13-inch baking pan. Combine teriyaki sauce, soy sauce and sesame oil in shallow bowl. Dip chicken pieces in butter, then in sauce. Arrange in baking pan; sprinkle with sesame seeds. Bake uncovered for 1 hour at 350°, basting with juices several times.

Optional: Set chicken aside; remove most of grease from pan. Thicken remaining juices with a roux made of 1 tablespoon flour and 1 tablespoon butter combined. Add chicken broth or white wine and reduce to desired consistency. Serve over noodles or rice and chicken.

CHICKEN FLORENTINE

An exciting blend of textures and flavors.

8 chicken thighs

4 tablespoons butter

Salt and pepper

1 medium onion, cut in thin slices

2 cloves garlic, crushed

1 (10-ounce) package frozen chopped spinach

¼ teaspoon salt

1 teaspoon basil

¼ cup Parmesan cheese, grated

8 ounces spaghetti or linguini, cooked and drained

Serves 4 to 6.

Sauté chicken in melted butter until browned on both sides. Season with salt and pepper to taste. Add onion and garlic; cover and cook 5 to 15 minutes or until almost done. Remove chicken.

Place spinach in same skillet; add ¼ teaspoon salt and the basil. Cover and cook for 10 minutes, piercing spinach with a fork and separating it as it cooks; stir to combine with onions and garlic. Return chicken to skillet; sprinkle with Parmesan cheese. Cover and cook gently for 5 to 10 minutes. Meanwhile, prepare pasta; drain well.

Mound pasta evenly on heated platter. Arrange spinach and chicken attractively on top.

FAVORITE CHICKEN HASH

2 chicken breasts, broiled

2 strips of bacon, crisp

½ small onion, sautéed

2 tablespoons butter

½ teaspoon lemon juice

Salt and pepper

2 tablespoons sour cream

1 teaspoon dry sherry

Serves 2.

Cut chicken in fine strips, crumble bacon and combine with the onion, butter, lemon juice and seasonings. Sauté until thoroughly heated in the butter. Shortly before serving add the sherry and sour cream.

Do not allow to cook after adding the two last ingredients. Just heat through.

Bob Hope

"Thanks for the Memories" from the thousands of U.S. troops he has entertained throughout the world. "The nation's favorite and most beloved entertainer" by Senate decree.

COQ AU VIN

A variation of a traditional French country meal.

2 frying chickens, 2 to 2½ pounds each

Flour, seasoned with salt and pepper

2 to 4 tablespoons fresh ginger, grated

¼ to ½ cup butter

12 tiny white onions

2 cloves garlic, crushed

1 bay leaf

Parsley, chopped

1 stalk celery, leaves and all, chopped

1 cup fresh mushrooms, sliced if large

¼ teaspoon marjoram

¼ teaspoon rosemary

½ cup chicken stock

3 cups Burgundy

Serves 6.

Cut chicken into pieces; dredge in seasoned flour with ginger added. Brown in butter in a heavy skillet. Add remaining ingredients except Burgundy; simmer about 8 minutes. Transfer to a casserole; add Burgundy; cover tightly. Bake at 350° for 1 to 1½ hours. Remove bay leaf before serving.

TAJEIN JAGA ZITOON

Sweet and spicy chicken.

1 large fryer, cut in serving pieces

2 tablespoons butter

1 teaspoon salt

½ teaspoon paprika

Pepper to taste

1 medium onion, sliced

3 tablespoons orange juice concentrate, undiluted

2 tablespoons honey

1 tablespoon lemon juice

½ teaspoon ground ginger

2 whole cloves

¼ teaspoon nutmeg

¼ cup ripe olives, sliced

Serves 4.

Brown chicken in melted butter seasoned with salt, paprika and pepper. Remove chicken to a Dutch oven or casserole. Sauté onions until limp in the skillet in which chicken was browned; spoon over chicken.

Combine remaining ingredients. Pour over chicken and bake, covered at 350° for 1 hour or until chicken is tender.

This recipe may be doubled or even quadrupled.

CHICKEN WINGS WITH PIQUANT SAUCE

The sauce in this recipe is excellent with pork chops, spareribs, Cornish game hens and a variety of other meat and poultry cuts.

3 to 4 pounds chicken wings

1 package dry onion soup mix

1 (10-ounce) jar apricot preserves

1 (8-ounce) bottle Russian dressing

Makes 21 to 28 pieces.

Trim tips off chicken wings. Place remaining sections in baking pan. Combine remaining ingredients and pour over chicken. Bake at 325° for 1½ hours, turning and basting at 45 minutes.

SOUR CREAM CHICKEN ENCHILADAS

Travels well to potlucks, tailgates, ski, boat or beach weekends.

3½ cups sour cream

2 or more cups cooked chicken or turkey, shredded

1 (8-ounce) can mushroom stems and pieces, drained

1 (4-ounce) can chopped green chiles, drained

¾ cup green onions, chopped

1 teaspoon chili powder

½ teaspoon salt

¼ to ½ teaspoon garlic powder

¼ teaspoon pepper

Salad oil

12 corn tortillas

1½ cups (6 ounces) sharp Cheddar cheese, grated

Serves 6.

Spread 1 cup sour cream in a lightly greased 9 x 13-inch baking pan. In 2 quart saucepan, combine chicken, mushrooms, green chiles, onions and seasonings. Cook over low heat, stirring occasionally, just until heated through.

Heat ½ inch of oil in an 8-inch skillet. Fry tortillas one at a time, just a few seconds on each side, to soften. Drain on paper towels.

For each enchilada spread about ¼ cup chicken mixture in center of a tortilla. Fold sides over filling, overlapping. Place seam side down in sour cream in baking pan.

Preheat oven to 350°. Spread remaining sour cream over enchiladas, then sprinkle with cheese. Bake 15 to 20 minutes or until cheese is melted and enchiladas are heated through.

CHICKEN LIVERS CARAMEL

An unusual combination that is surprisingly delicious.

1 pound chicken livers

6 tablespoons butter

⅓ cup brown sugar

2 tablespoons sherry or Marsala (optional)

Serves 4 to 6.

Sauté chicken livers in butter until barely done; do not overcook. Sprinkle brown sugar over livers; toss gently until caramelized. If desired, add wine. Pour any sauce over livers to serve.

CHICKEN LIVERS IN SOY SAUCE

A delectable way to cook chicken livers.

¼ cup soy sauce

2 tablespoons dry sherry

2 tablespoons brown sugar

¼ teaspoon ground ginger

3 tablespoons butter, divided

1 large onion, thinly sliced

½ cup mushrooms, sliced

1 pound fresh chicken livers

Flour

Serves 3 to 4.

Combine first four ingredients in small bowl; set aside. Melt 2 tablespoons butter in large skillet. Sauté onions and mushrooms until tender; remove with slotted spoon and set aside. Add last tablespoon butter to skillet and heat. Dredge livers lightly in flour; sauté until done. Add mushrooms, onions and soy mixture; heat thoroughly. Taste and correct seasoning; add salt and pepper if desired.

LEMON HAZELNUT STUFFING

A versatile dressing for a roasting chicken or boneless breasts, pork tenderloin or chops.

¾ cup onion, chopped

¾ cup celery, chopped

4 tablespoons butter

2 cups Pepperidge Farm seasoned dry crumb stuffing

½ cup hazelnuts, toasted and coarsely chopped

¾ teaspoon dried thyme

1 to 2 teaspoons lemon rind, finely grated

½ to ¾ teaspoon freshly grated nutmeg

½ cup hot water or broth

Basting sauce (optional):

3 tablespoons dry white wine

3 tablespoons orange juice

1 tablespoon butter

Makes 4 cups.

Sauté onion and celery in butter. Add remaining ingredients; toss well in pan to heat through. Cool before using. If desired, baste with sauce while baking.

CORN BREAD STUFFING

A versatile dressing for turkey or other poultry; try with pork chops too.

½ pound pork sausage

1 large onion, chopped

1 stalk celery, chopped

1 tablespoon butter

8 cups corn bread, coarsely crumbled

1 (8-ounce) can water chestnuts, drained and chopped

2 eggs, lightly beaten

2 teaspoons salt

½ teaspoon pepper

2 tablespoons parsley, chopped

1 teaspoon thyme

½ teaspoon sage

Water or broth to moisten, if needed

Makes 10 cups.

Fry sausage; crumble and drain. Sauté onion and celery in butter until soft. Combine with corn bread, sausage and remaining ingredients.

Lightly stuff turkey cavity. Bake extra stuffing in buttered, covered casserole at 325° for 45 minutes. Moisten with juices from turkey if desired.

MUSHROOM STUFFING ALMONDINE

This stands on its own as an accompaniment.

6 strips bacon, cut in small pieces

½ cup butter or margarine (1 cube)

1 cup onion, chopped

1 cup celery, sliced

1½ cups fresh mushrooms, sliced

1 teaspoon poultry seasoning

¼ teaspoon pepper

1 chicken bouillon cube

½ cup hot water

6 cups day-old bread cubes, unseasoned

⅔ cup almonds, chopped and toasted

1 apple, peeled, cored and chopped

Serves 6 to 8.

In a large skillet, cook bacon until crisp. Remove bacon; add onion, celery and mushrooms; sauté until tender. Add butter, poultry seasoning and pepper, stirring until butter melts; add bouillon cube dissolved in hot water. Pour entire mixture over bread, tossing to moisten evenly. Add almonds, apple and reserved bacon; mix lightly. Turn into a 2-quart baking dish. Bake at 350° about 40 minutes or until lightly toasted on top.

SOLE FLORENTINE

Sour cream adds a nice tang to the spinach and fish.

3 (10-ounce) packages frozen chopped spinach

2 cups sour cream

3 tablespoons flour

½ cup green onions (including tops), finely chopped

Juice of 1 lemon

2 teaspoons salt

2 tablespoons butter

1½ to 2 pounds petrale sole fillets

Paprika

Serves 6 to 8.

Cook spinach as package directs; drain well. Blend sour cream, flour, onions, lemon juice and salt. Add half sour cream mixture to spinach. Spread this mixture evenly over bottom of a shallow 9 x 13-inch baking dish. Place sole on spinach bed, dot with butter. Spread remaining sour cream mixture evenly over sole. Dust lightly with paprika. (Can be refrigerated at this point.) Bake at 375° for 25 minutes or until fish is done.

FILLET OF SOLE JOINVILLE

A "Gourmet Gala" entry.

8 to 10 sole fillets

1¾ pounds raw salmon (weight after skin and bones removed)

2 egg whites

1 cup light cream

2 teaspoons salt

1 teaspoon pepper

1 teaspoon dry tarragon

2 tablespoons parsley, chopped

Shrimp and mushrooms for garnish

Serves 6.

Wash sole fillets in lemon juice and water; dry and set aside. Brush a 10-inch ring mold with oil. Line mold with fillets overlapping, skin side on bottom of pan and narrow ends in center. Set aside.

Grind raw salmon in food processor. Beat egg whites into salmon. Slowly beat in cream, salt, pepper, tarragon and parsley; beat hard in food processor to mix well. Spoon into fish-lined mold and fold fillet ends over to cover top. Cover with buttered foil, parchment paper or typewriter paper; set in hot water bath.

Bake in 350° preheated oven for 25 to 30 minutes. When done, let stand 5 minutes before unmolding. Run knife around edges and unmold on rack over a pan to catch juices for sauce.

Transfer to platter. Place shrimp and mushrooms which have been sautéed in center of mold, or garnish as desired. Serve with Sauce Buerre Blanc.

SAUCE BUERRE BLANC

¼ to ½ cup fish juices

½ cup shallots, chopped

1 cup dry white wine

½ cup heavy cream

½ pound butter (2 cubes)

Egg yolk (optional)

Makes about 1½ cups.

Combine first 3 ingredients; reduce by half (will not burn, so may be cooked fast). When reduced, add cream and cook on high heat until the mixture coats the back of a spoon.

Remove from heat and let sauce settle a bit. Cool down and start adding soft butter; will take up to ½ pound butter. If this separates, throw in a small chunk of COLD butter and whisk in. Egg yolk or potato flour may be used to thicken, but this is not necessary.

HAMMER'S SUPERB BARBECUED SALMON

A unique preparation for our wonderful Northwest salmon.

6 to 8 pound whole salmon

¼ pound melted butter

¼ cup olive oil

4 garlic cloves, crushed

1½ teaspoon Worcestershire

1 teaspoon onion salt

2 dashes Tabasco

¼ cup dry white wine or dry sherry

Juice of ½ lemon

1 tablespoon stone-ground mustard

4 tablespoons honey or white wine jelly

Serves 8 to 10

Clean, scale and split salmon on belly side to the dorsal fin, being careful not to split down backbone.

Combine all remaining ingredients except honey for sauce.

Lay "butterflied" fish skin side down, on pre-heated, medium-hot, greased barbecue grill. Pierce fish with fork in several places; sprinkle liberally with freshly ground pepper. Generously brush prepared sauce on fish. Close barbecue lid. Continue brushing sauce on fish every 5 minutes during cooking. Fish is done when it flakes easily, approximately 20 to 30 minutes. Do not overcook.

During last 5 minutes, brush honey or melted white wine jelly on fish to glaze.

HERB TOPPED FISH

The flavorful topping keeps fish from becoming dry.

8 (1 to 1½-inch thick) pieces of halibut or other white fish, deboned

¾ cup mayonnaise

½ cup sour cream

½ cup freshly grated Parmesan cheese

4 tablespoons chives, chopped

2 tablespoons parsley, chopped

½ teaspoon onion salt

½ teaspoon dried dill

½ teaspoon dry mustard

Fresh ground pepper to taste

Serves 8.

Place uncooked fish in a buttered shallow baking dish.

Blend all remaining ingredients by hand. Spread mixture on top of fillets. Bake at 350° for 20 minutes or until fish flakes.

SEATTLE BAKED HALIBUT

This recipe respects the flavor of the halibut.

2 pounds fresh or frozen halibut steaks

1 teaspoon salt

2 tablespoons butter

4 ounces fresh mushrooms, sliced

1 cup sour cream

¼ cup white wine

Dash paprika

Lemon wedges

Parsley

Serves 4 to 6.

Place halibut in a buttered shallow baking dish. Sprinkle with salt. Bake at 425° for 10 minutes.

Melt butter in sauce pan and sauté mushrooms. Remove from heat, add sour cream and wine. Pour sauce over halibut. Sprinkle with paprika.

Return to oven and bake at 375° for 10 minutes or until done. Serve with lemon wedges; garnish with parsley.

BROILED HALIBUT WITH HERB BUTTER

This savory blend of herbs will delight guests and family.

2 pounds halibut steaks (1-inch thick), fresh or frozen

⅓ cup butter or margarine

2 tablespoons onion, minced

½ teaspoon salt

1 garlic clove, minced

¼ teaspoon black pepper, coarsely ground

¼ teaspoon dried thyme

⅛ teaspoon dried tarragon

¼ teaspoon dried basil

¼ teaspoon dried parsley

1 tablespoon lemon juice

Serves 4 to 6.

If halibut is frozen, let stand 30 minutes at room temperature. Place halibut in foil-lined broiler pan without rack. Cream butter with onion and seasonings. Add lemon juice, little by little, mixing thoroughly after each addition. Spread half the herb butter over fish.

Broil under preheated broiler, 2 inches from source of heat, 3 minutes for fresh halibut, or 5 minutes for partially thawed frozen halibut. With pancake turner, carefully turn fish; spread remaining herb butter over surface.

Return to broiler; broil 3 to 5 minutes longer or until fish flakes easily when tested with a fork; do not overcook. Remove to serving platter and spoon sauce in broiler pan over fish.

HALIBUT LOAF WITH ALMOND OR LOBSTER CREAM SAUCE

"This recipe was given to me many years ago by my Norwegian cook. Delicious for entertaining and easy. Sometimes I double the recipe and freeze for a later date."

2 pounds fresh halibut

1 onion

10 slices white bread

1½ cups cream

4 egg whites, beaten stiff

Salt and pepper

Serves 8.

Remove skin and bones from fish, then grind fish and onion together (I do it in a Cuisinart).

Remove crust from bread and soak in cream. Mix fish with soaked bread; add salt and pepper to taste. Fold in beaten egg whites. Put in a greased bread pan or Pyrex loaf and bake like custard in pan of water in a 350° oven for 1 hour. Remove from pan to platter. Pour cream sauce with lobster meat, or cream sauce with sliced almonds on top to serve.

Phyllis Thaxter

Phyllis Thaxter

A screen and television actress well known for her role as the mother in the "Lassie" series.

SALMON CAKES

Light in texture; try with Dilled Sour Cream.

1 (1-pound) can salmon

1 egg

⅓ to ½ cup onion, minced

½ cup flour

1½ teaspoon baking powder

¼ teaspoon salt or garlic salt

⅛ teaspoon pepper

½ teaspoon lemon juice

½ teaspoon Italian herbs, crushed (optional)

2 tablespoons reserved salmon liquid

Serves 6.

Drain salmon, reserve liquid. Remove all skin and bones. In bowl, flake salmon, add egg and onion; mix until sticky. Add remaining ingredients and mix well. Shape into 6 patties; dust lightly with flour. Fry in oil until golden brown. Serve warm, garnished with parsley, greens or a cream sauce.

Leftover salmon or two (7-ounce) cans tuna may be substituted.

SALMON WHIFFLE

An easy salmon loaf that's as delightful as its name.

2 cups milk

24 soda crackers, crushed

1 small onion, chopped

½ green pepper, chopped

4 tablespoons butter, melted

1 (16-ounce) can salmon, flaked, or 2 cups
  fresh cooked salmon

1 tablespoon Worcestershire or A-1

Salt and pepper to taste

4 eggs, well-beaten

Serves 4.

Soak crackers in milk. Add remaining ingredients, except eggs; combine thoroughly. Fold in eggs. Pour into buttered casserole and bake, uncovered, at 350° for 45 minutes.

CUE: For cooking scallops: Rinse and dry carefully. Cooking time varies according to size; scallops are done when they become opaque and lose their translucency; be careful not to overcook.

SCALLOPS À LA JETTY

A fine blend of flavors; spoon sauce over freshly cooked pasta to serve.

3 tablespoons butter or margarine

1 clove garlic, minced, or ¼ teaspoon garlic salt

1 pound medium scallops

½ pound mushrooms, sliced

½ cup green onions, chopped

¼ cup sauterne or white wine

Serves 2 to 3.

Over medium heat, sauté garlic in butter. Add scallops, mushrooms and green onions; sauté, stirring, for 3 minutes. Add wine and cook 2 minutes more or until scallops are done; do not overcook. Serve with lemon wedges.

Prawns can be substituted for scallops.

SCALLOPS DIJONNAISE

Guaranteed to be delicious, and with quick preparation.

1 pound fresh scallops

3 tablespoons butter, divided

1 small clove garlic, crushed

2 tablepsoons shallots or green onions, finely chopped

½ cup dry white wine

½ cup whipping cream

1 tablespoon Dijon mustard

Salt, pepper and lemon juice to taste

Fresh parsley, chopped

Serves 4.

Rinse and dry scallops. Melt 2 tablespoons butter in skillet and sauté scallops briefly; be careful not to overcook. Remove scallops to a warm serving dish. Pour out any darkened butter from the pan. Add remaining butter with garlic and shallots; cook gently for 30 seconds; do not brown.

Deglaze the pan with wine; reduce to about 2 tablespoons. Add cream; cook gently until thickened. Without allowing sauce to boil, whisk in mustard; add salt, pepper and lemon juice to taste. Return scallops to pan and toss with sauce to reheat. Serve topped with chopped parsley.

COQUILLES ST. CHARLES

Requires some last minute preparation, but it's well worth it.

2 tablespoons butter

¼ teaspoon saffron

2 tablespoons shallots, minced

2 pounds large scallops

2 tablespoons cognac

2 tablespoons dry vermouth

1 tablespoon lemon juice

1 cup heavy cream

¼ pound mushrooms, sliced

1 large tomato, peeled, seeded and coarsely chopped

½ teaspoon salt

½ teaspoon white pepper

4 tablespoons freshly grated Parmesan cheese

Serves 6.

Melt butter in large flame-proof casserole; add saffron and shallots and sauté until softened. Add scallops, cognac, vermouth and lemon juice. Poach scallops, covered, for about 8 minutes or until done. Transfer scallops to a heated dish; keep warm in oven.

Add cream to pan and reduce one third. Add mushrooms, tomatoes, salt and pepper; heat through. Pour sauce over individual servings; top with Parmesan cheese. Serve hot.

SCALLOPS AND SHRIMP OSWEGO

A variation of Coquilles St. Jacques which has become a "house specialty".

¾ pound fresh scallops, bite sized

1 cup dry white wine

2 tablespoons lemon juice

½ teaspoon salt

¼ teaspoon white pepper

1 or 2 bay leaves

¾ pound small Pacific shrimp

½ pound small fresh mushrooms, sliced

4 tablespoons butter or margarine

6 tablespoons flour

¼ teaspoon dry mustard

2¼ cups liquid (reserved wine plus half & half or evaporated milk)

¼ pound Swiss or Cheddar cheese, grated, or a combination

¼ cup fresh parsley, finely chopped

2 or 3 green onions, very thinly sliced

Worcestershire and Tabasco to taste

Buttered fresh bread crumbs

Serves 6.

Combine wine, lemon juice, salt, pepper and bay leaves in a 2-quart saucepan. Bring to a boil; reduce heat and simmer 2 minutes. Add scallops and simmer 2 minutes; do not over-cook; remove and set aside. Add mushrooms to the wine; simmer 1 to 2 minutes. Drain, reserving liquid. Discard bay leaves.

Melt butter in same saucepan. Add flour and mustard; blend thoroughly, stirring constantly over low heat 1 to 2 minutes. Add liquid all at once, cook, stirring constantly, until sauce just starts to bubble. Remove from heat; add cheese and stir to melt. Add parsley and green onions.

Add scallops, mushrooms and shrimp. Taste and correct seasoning, adding Worcestershire, Tabasco and more lemon juice, salt and pepper if desired. Add any liquid that may have accumulated around scallops. Thin with milk if necessary.

Grease 6 individual casseroles. Divide mixture evenly among them. Top generously with fresh buttered bread crumbs. Bake in 350° oven until mixture is hot and crumbs are golden.

SAUTÉED SEAFOOD NORMANDY

Serve in individual scallop shells for eye, scent and taste appeal; a 5-star winner.

2 tablespoons butter

6 shallots or 3 green onions, finely chopped

⅓ cup cider vinegar

Salt and freshly ground pepper to taste

1¼ cup whipping cream

¼ cup oil

1½ to 2 pounds scallops or shrimp, shelled and deveined

Serves 6.

Heat butter in a skillet. Add shallots; sauté until golden. Add vinegar; reduce slowly until no liquid is left. Add salt, pepper and cream. Reduce until approximately ¾ cup cream remains. Set aside.

In another skillet heat oil until very hot. Add seafood and sauté quickly. Remove and serve with shallot vinegar reduction.

CASSEROLE OF SNAPPER AND SHRIMP

A versatile recipe; you can use seafood of the season and vary the cheese to your taste.

1¼ pounds red snapper fillets

½ pound small shrimp

3 ounces noodles

2 tablespoons butter

2 tablespoons flour

2⅔ cups milk

1 teaspoon salt

⅛ teaspoon pepper

¼ teaspoon paprika

1½ cup cheese, grated

1 teaspoon Worcestershire

2 tablespoons lemon juice

1½ cup bread crumbs

Serves 6 to 8.

Poach snapper only until it loses its transparency; don't overcook. Flake and combine with shrimp. Cook noodles in boiling salted water; drain and rinse.

Make sauce of butter, flour and milk. Add seasonings and ½ cup cheese; stir until smooth. Add Worcestershire and lemon juice.

Combine sauce with fish and pour into greased casserole. Sprinkle with remaining cheese and bread crumbs. Bake at 325° for 1 hour or until nicely browned.

If desired, finely chopped green pepper, celery and mushrooms sautéed in butter may be added before baking. Shrimp (1¾ pounds) may be used in place of snapper and shrimp combination.

SHRIMP AND ARTICHOKE CASSEROLE

3¾ pounds jumbo prawns (or equivalent chicken breasts, lobster or combination of any of them)

1 bay leaf

6 or 8 peppercorns

¾ pound fresh mushrooms

½ pound butter

Scant ¾ cup flour

Salt and pepper to taste

1½ cups milk

2 cups whipping cream

¾ cup good dry sherry

½ teaspoon Worcestershire

3 (14-ounce) cans artichoke hearts

¾ cup freshly grated Parmesan cheese

Paprika

Serves 12.

In salted water, simmer prawns with bay leaf and peppercorns, 5 to 15 minutes, depending on size or until just tender. In large pan sauté mushrooms in butter 3 or 4 minutes. Add flour and salt and pepper to taste; stir until flour absorbs butter. Add milk and cream and cook until thickened, stirring constantly. Add sherry and Worcestershire. Add artichoke hearts, then prawns.

Put in large casserole. Sprinkle Parmesan cheese on top plus paprika for color. Bake at 375° for 30 to 60 minutes, depending on temperature of casserole when put into oven.

"Cues" from the Leydens:

1. Artichokes must be well drained. Squeeze them individually, gently, to remove liquid; cut in thirds or halves depending on size.

2. The larger the prawns, the better the texture for this dish. Cooking them in advance and chilling before adding seems to help retain crisp texture.

3. You may want to cut prawns in half if used in combination with cut up, boned chicken breasts.

4. Casserole is best when made a day in advance.

Alice and Norman Leyden

Alice and Norman Leyden

Alice is a score recorder, an arranger and librarian for the Oregon Symphony Pops. Norman is the conductor of the Oregon Symphony Pops and a former member of the Glenn Miller band.

GREEN NOODLE CASSEROLE

The girls are coming to lunch, and this is simply delicious.

1 (8-ounce) package spinach noodles

1 pound shrimp, crab or chicken, cooked

1 bunch green onions, thinly sliced

1 can water chestnuts, sliced and drained

¼ cup green pepper, diced

¾ cup mayonnaise

¾ cup sour cream

¼ teaspoon Worcestershire

1 cup Cheddar cheese, grated

Serves 4.

Cook noodles and place in greased 2-quart casserole. Place seafood, onions, water chestnuts and green pepper on top. Combine mayonnaise, sour cream and Worcestershire; pour over seafood and noodles. Sprinkle top with grated cheese. Bake at 350° for approximately 30 minutes. This can be made ahead with the cheese added just before baking.

Do not microwave; bake in conventional oven.

BAKED SHRIMP AND LEMON SLICES

Don't let all the lemons scare you; they add a great zesty flavor.

2 to 3 pounds cooked shrimp

1 cup cooked rice

1 cup sharp cheese, grated

1 can condensed mushroom soup, undiluted

½ cup green pepper, chopped

½ cup green onion, chopped

½ cup celery, chopped

½ cup (1 cube) butter

8 lemons, sliced very thin

Serves 6 to 8.

Mix first 4 ingredients together. Sauté green pepper, onion, and celery in butter. Add to shrimp mixture. Put mixture in long flat casserole and completely cover top with sliced lemons. Cook, covered, at 375° for about 20 minutes. May be frozen before baking.

FAT MAN'S SHRIMP

A great hit, even with non-seafood lovers.

2 (10-ounce) packages frozen chopped spinach

½ pound fresh mushrooms, sliced

1 cup sour cream

2 (10½-ounce) cans cream of mushroom soup, undiluted

½ cup freshly grated Parmesan cheese

½ teaspoon dry mustard

3 cups shrimp, cooked

Grated coconut or bread crumbs

Serves 6.

Defrost spinach; drain and squeeze out moisture. In saucepan, sauté mushrooms. Combine sour cream and mushroom soup; add to mushrooms. Add cheese and mustard. Heat until warm. Add shrimp.

Place half of spinach in a shallow 1½ to 2-quart casserole, then half of shrimp mixture. Repeat. Sprinkle grated coconut or coarse bread crumbs on top. Bake uncovered at 350° for 30 minutes.

SCAMPI IN VERMOUTH

Serve as a first course or as an entrée.

1 pound prawns or scampi, shelled and deveined

¼ cup olive oil

1 clove garlic, crushed

Dash pepper

¼ teaspoon salt

¼ cup dry vermouth

Fresh parsley, chopped

Lemon wedges

Serves 4.

Sauté prawns in olive oil about 3 minutes. Add garlic, salt, pepper and vermouth; cook until liquid is almost gone. Serve with chopped parsley and lemon wedges.

Excellent with hot, crunchy French bread.

PAELLA

½ teaspoon saffron

4 chicken legs and 4 thighs, separated

½ cup oil

2 cloves garlic, chopped

¼ pound fresh pork, diced

1 or 2 medium tomatoes, peeled, seeded and cut up

A few fresh green beans

2 or 3 artichoke hearts, marinated

1 teaspoon paprika

1½ cups long grain white rice

1½ teaspoons salt

4 cups boiling fish stock, bottled clam juice, or chicken broth

10 to 12 raw shrimp, unshelled

10 to 12 raw clams, unshelled

8 shrimp in shell

Pimiento strips

Serves 6.

Pound saffron in a mortar; soak in small amount of wine or stock; set aside. Brown chicken in oil and garlic; add pork and brown thoroughly; add tomatoes, green beans, artichoke hearts, paprika and rice. Cook until rice is coated with oil. Add salt, stock and saffron; cook until rice is just beginning to get tender. Add shrimps and clams; cook until rice is tender, the liquid is absorbed and the clams have opened.

Cook the 8 shrimps in shell: bring pot of water to rolling boil, add shrimps and cook until they turn pink; drain. Use with pimiento strips as a garnish.

OYSTERS BENSON

A palate pleaser for a light supper, originally from a reknowned Portland hotel.

2 tablespoons unsalted butter

¼ cup green onions, chopped

Green pepper, chopped (optional)

2 (10-ounce) jars small oysters, rinsed and dried

¼ cup white wine or vermouth

1 teaspoon curry powder

2 cups sour cream

2 to 3 cups hot steamed rice

Lemon wedges

Fresh parsley

Serves 4 to 6.

Melt butter in large saute pan; add green onions and sauté without overcooking. Add oysters and brown lightly; add wine and curry powder; gently simmer until oysters are firm. Remove oysters to a warm plate; reduce the liquid by half. Stir in sour cream until smooth. Return oysters to the pan; gently cook just until sour cream and oysters are hot.

Serve over hot rice. Garnish with lemon wedges and fresh parsley. May also be served on a bed of sautéed spinach.

BLINTZ SOUFFLÉ

Everyone who tastes this wants the recipe. It may be prepared the day before serving and baked in the morning.

Filling:

1 (8-ounce) package cream cheese, softened

2 cups small curd cottage cheese

2 egg yolks

1 tablespoon sugar

1 teaspoon vanilla

Batter:

½ cup butter (1 cube), softened

⅓ cup sugar

6 eggs

1½ cups sour cream

½ cup orange juice

1 cup flour

2 teaspoons baking powder

Serves 6 to 8.

Combine filling ingredients and blend well; set aside.

In a blender or mixer bowl combine batter ingredients until well blended. Pour half the batter into a buttered 9 x 13-inch baking pan. Drop filling by heaping spoonfuls over the batter, then spread gently with a spatula; filling may mix slightly with the batter. Pour remaining batter on top. Unbaked soufflé may be covered and refrigerated several hours or overnight; bring to room temperature before baking.

Bake, uncovered, at 350° for 50 to 60 minutes or until puffed and golden. Serve at once with sweetened sour cream with a bit of cinnamon added or Blueberry Syrup or strawberry or raspberry jam.

BLUEBERRY SYRUP

1 (15-ounce) can blueberries in light syrup

½ cup light corn syrup

½ teaspoon lemon juice

Dash salt

Dash cinnamon

1 tablespoon cornstarch

1 tablespoon water

Makes 2 cups.

Combine blueberries, corn syrup, lemon juice, salt and cinnamon in saucepan; bring to a boil. Combine cornstarch and water; stir into syrup and cook, stirring constantly, until clear and thickened. Remove from heat and let stand 5 to 10 minutes. Serve warm; may be reheated.

FANCY EGG SCRAMBLE

Everyone wanted seconds according to our tester.

1 cup Canadian bacon or cooked ham, diced

¼ cup green onion, chopped

3 tablespoons butter or margarine

12 beaten eggs

2 tablespoons butter or margarine

2 tablespoons flour

½ teaspoon salt

⅛ teaspoon pepper

2 cups milk

1 cup sharp Cheddar cheese, grated

½ pound mushrooms, sliced and sautéed

4 teaspoons butter or margarine, melted

2 cups soft bread crumbs

⅛ teaspoon paprika

Serves 6 to 8.

In large skillet, sauté Canadian bacon or ham and onion in butter until onion is tender but not brown. Add eggs; scramble just until set.

Make a cheese sauce: melt the 2 tablespoons butter over low heat; blend in flour, salt and pepper. Cook over low heat, stirring, until mixture is smooth; slowly stir in milk; bring to a simmer, stirring constantly until thickened. Stir in cheese and heat until melted.

Fold mushrooms and egg mixture into cheese sauce. Pour into a 9 x 13-inch baking dish. Combine remaining melted butter, bread crumbs and paprika; sprinkle over egg mixture. Cover and refrigerate overnight if desired. Bake, uncovered, at 350° for 30 minutes.

SAVORY EGGS IN CASSEROLE

This may be prepared the day before; bake just before serving.

12 hard cooked eggs, cut in half

½ pound ham, minced

1 teaspoon vinegar

1 teaspoon dry mustard

¼ teaspoon black pepper

Dash cayenne pepper

¾ cup melted butter

3 tablespoons butter

3 tablespoons flour

¼ teaspoon salt

⅛ teaspoon black pepper

1½ cups milk

1 pound medium Cheddar cheese, grated

1 pound bacon, fried, drained and crumbled

Serves 8 to 10.

Cool cooked eggs, remove yolks and mash. To yolks add next six ingredients. Stuff egg white halves with yolk mixture; place in buttered 9 x 11-inch casserole.

Make a white sauce: melt the 3 tablespoons butter over low heat in heavy saucepan; blend in flour and seasoning, stirring. Cook over low heat, continuing to stir, until mixture is smooth and bubbly. Remove from heat, slowly stir in milk. Bring to a boil, stirring constantly; boil 1 minute or until thick. Add cheese to white sauce and heat to melt. Pour over eggs; top with crumbled bacon.

Can be refrigerated overnight. Bring to room temperature; bake at 350° for 20 minutes or until heated through.

EASTER EGG BRUNCH CASSEROLE

Even people who usually don't like eggs enjoy this.

2 (12-ounce) cans artichokes, drained and cut in quarters

2 cans cream of mushroom soup, undiluted

1 tablespoon onion, minced

¼ cup pale dry sherry

1 bay leaf

½ teaspoon garlic salt

¼ teaspoon salt

White pepper to taste

2 cups ham, diced in ½-inch cubes

8 to 10 hard-cooked eggs

Cheddar cheese, grated

Serves 8.

Heat artichokes, soup, onion, sherry and seasonings in saucepan. Spread the ham cubes in a 3-quart flat casserole; pour heated mixture over ham. Cut eggs in half through their "waists" and arrange in casserole mixture so only the "eyes" are exposed. Cover with a layer of grated Cheddar. Bake at 400° for 25 to 30 minutes, until bubbly and a bit browned.

May substitute shrimp for ham, and grated Meunster for Cheddar.

TOP OF THE STOVE CHEESE SOUFFLÉ

A soufflé that holds forever — it's magic!

4 tablespoons butter

2 heaping tablespoons flour

1 cup milk

Salt and white pepper to taste

½ pound medium Cheddar cheese, grated

4 egg yolks, beaten

4 egg whites, beaten stiff

Serves 4 to 6.

Melt butter in top of double boiler; add flour, stirring until smooth. Add milk, continuing to stir, then add salt and pepper; stir until mixture is smooth and creamy. Add grated cheese. Fold in egg yolks, then egg whites.

Cook, covered, 45 minutes on medium low heat. Time may vary according to size of double boiler. When done, the lid will push off top of pan.

Recipe can be doubled or divided easily. This soufflé holds well, even until the next day. It can be served plain or with curry, crab or mushroom sauce.

President Reagan's Favorite Macaroni and Cheese

½ lb. macaroni
1 t. butter
1 egg, beaten
1 t. salt

1 t. dry mustard
3 C. grated cheese, sharp
1 C. milk

Boil macaroni in water until tender and drain thoroughly. Stir in butter and egg. Mix mustard and salt with 1 tablespoon hot water and add to milk. Add cheese leaving enough to sprinkle on top. Pour into buttered casserole, add milk, sprinkle with cheese. Bake at 350° for about 45 minutes or until custard is set and top is crusty.

Nancy Reagan

SAUSAGE SOUFFLÉ

The texture of a soufflé with the ease of a strata.

4 slices buttered bread, cubed

2 eggs, lightly beaten

1¾ cups Swiss cheese, grated

2 teaspoons dry mustard

½ teaspoon salt

½ teaspoon pepper

2 cups milk

1 (4-ounce) can green chiles, drained and chopped

1 pound bulk sausage, cooked and drained (Jimmy Dean, if possible)

Serves 5 to 6.

In a large bowl, add all ingredients except cooked meat; mix well. Refrigerate at least 2 hours or overnight. When ready to bake, add cooked meat. Pour mixture into shallow casserole or soufflé dish. Bake at 350° for 50 to 60 minutes.

Five times this recipe will fill two 9 x 13-inch pans.

MUSHROOM GÂTEAU

With lighted candles, this makes a spectacular first course "birthday cake" for anyone avoiding sweets.

16 crêpes

Filling:

½ cup green onions and tops, chopped

4 tablespoons butter

1 pound mushrooms, finely chopped

2 tablespoons Madeira

2 tablespoons Parmesan cheese, grated

4 hard-cooked eggs, finely chopped

1 tablespoon lemon juice

½ teaspoon salt

Freshly ground pepper

Sauce:

4 tablespoons butter

6 tablespoons flour

2 cups milk

1 to 1¼ cups heavy cream

½ teaspoon salt

⅛ teaspoon white pepper

¼ cup Parmesan cheese, grated

Serves 6 to 8 as a luncheon dish, or 10 to 12 as a first course.

Make crêpes, using any standard recipe.

To prepare filling, cook green onion in butter until soft. Add mushrooms. Cover and cook 5 minutes. Remove cover, add Madeira, increase heat and evaporate liquid. Transfer ingredients to a bowl. Add Parmesan cheese, eggs, lemon juice, salt and pepper.

To prepare sauce, melt butter. Stir in flour; cook 2 to 3 minutes. Add milk, cook until thick. Stir 8 tablespoons of sauce into prepared filling. To the remaining sauce add cream, salt, pepper and cheese.

To assemble layers, butter bottom of 9-inch glass pie plate. Place a crêpe on the bottom of plate. Spread with scant 2 tablespoons filling. Alternate crêpes and filling, ending with a crêpe. Spread ½ cup sauce over top and sides. Sprinkle with Parmesan cheese and dot with butter. The cake can be refrigerated overnight and baked just before serving, or it can be frozen and served at a later date. Thaw before baking.

Bake at 375° 15 to 25 minutes until delicately browned. Garnish with watercress, parsley or other greens. Cut in wedges and serve with extra sauce.

CRUSTLESS CRAB QUICHE

A good way to enjoy quiche without the added calories of pastry.

½ pound fresh mushrooms, thinly sliced

2 tablespoons butter or margarine

4 eggs

1 cup sour cream

1 cup small curd cottage cheese

½ cup Parmesan cheese, grated

¼ cup flour

1 teaspoon onion powder

¼ teaspoon salt

4 drops Tabasco sauce

½ pound Monterey Jack cheese, grated

6 ounces fresh or frozen crab or shrimp, well drained

Serves 6.

Sauté mushrooms in butter until tender; remove and drain well. In food processor combine eggs, sour cream, cottage cheese, Parmesan cheese, flour and seasonings. Process until eggs are frothy and ingredients well blended. Fold in mushrooms, Jack cheese and seafood.

Pour into greased 9 or 10-inch quiche or pie pan. Bake at 350° for 45 minutes or until golden brown on top and knife inserted comes out clean. Let stand 5 minutes before serving.

ALVARADO QUICHE

Don't pass this by; it's excellent for brunch, lunch or supper.

1 (9-inch) pie shell, partially baked

12 slices crisp bacon

1 cup ripe olives, sliced

1 cup Swiss cheese, grated

1 cup whipping cream

2 eggs, slightly beaten

Dash salt and pepper

Serves 6.

In bottom of pie shell, crumble bacon; add olives and cheese. Scald cream; add eggs, salt and pepper. Pour into crust; bake at 350° until custard is set, 20 to 30 minutes.

ARTICHOKE QUICHE

Fewer calories and less fat than most quiches.

1 (10-inch) unbaked pie shell

1 (14-ounce) can water pack artichokes

3 eggs

1 (8-ounce) package Neufchâtel cheese, softened

1 cup low-fat cottage cheese

¾ cup buttermilk

1 (2-inch) cube white cheese, grated (Meunster, Swiss or Mozzarella)

½ to 1 teaspoon salt

¼ teaspoon thyme

¼ teaspoon white pepper

¼ teaspoon Beau Monde seasoning

6 slices lean bacon, cooked and crumbled

Serves 4 to 6.

Drain artichokes, cut in quarters. Beat eggs; add Neufchâtel, cottage cheese and buttermilk. Add grated cheese. Stir in seasonings and crumbled bacon. Place artichokes in bottom of pie shell; pour cheese mixture over artichokes. Bake at 375° for 50 to 60 minutes or until toothpick comes out clean.

SPINACH QUICHE WITH PISTACHIOS

1 (10-inch) quiche pastry, unbaked

1 (10-ounce) package frozen chopped spinach, thawed

6 eggs

1 cup Ricotta cheese

2 cups half and half or whipping cream

1 cup Swiss cheese, grated

2 tablespoons Parmesan cheese, grated

½ cup pistachios, chopped

1 teaspoon salt

1½ teaspoons fresh dill, chopped, or 1 teaspoon dried dill weed

½ teaspoon white pepper

½ teaspoon sugar

Topping:

½ to 1 cup Provolone and Swiss cheese, grated

Paprika

Serves 8.

Prick pastry bottom and sides or use other method to prevent shrinking. Bake at 400° for 7 minutes. Remove from oven and reduce temperature to 350°.

Squeeze moisture out of spinach. In large mixing bowl, combine all ingredients except topping cheese and paprika, mixing well after each addition. Pour into partially baked pie shell; bake 45 to 55 minutes or until firm. Top with grated Provolone and Swiss cheeses; sprinkle with paprika. Return to oven just until cheese melts.

PAISANO PIE

Perfect for a family supper.

1 (10-ounce) package frozen chopped spinach, thawed

1 pound Ricotta cheese

¼ pound mushrooms, chopped

½ cup Swiss cheese, grated

½ cup Parmesan cheese, grated

¼ pound pepperoni sausage, thinly sliced

¼ cup onion, finely chopped

2 teaspoons prepared mustard

½ teaspoon oregano leaves

¼ teaspoon salt

Dash pepper

1 egg, slightly beaten

2 (9-inch) pie crusts, unbaked

Tomato sauce:

1 (15-ounce) can tomato sauce

½ teaspoon garlic salt

Dash pepper

1 teaspoon Italian herb seasoning

Serves 4 to 6.

Thoroughly drain spinach, pressing out as much moisture as possible. Blend with remaining filling ingredients. Roll out half of the pastry to line a 9-inch pie pan. Spread filling in pastry. Roll out remaining pastry for top crust; place on filling, trim and flute edge; prick top with a fork. Bake at 425° about 25 minutes or until crust is brown. Top with a tomato sauce made by heating canned tomato sauce with seasonings.

CHILES RELLENOS SOUFFLÉ

We tested three versions of this recipe, and this is the best one ever.

3 (4-ounce) cans whole green chiles

½ pound Cheddar cheese, grated

½ pound Monterey Jack cheese, grated

4 eggs, slightly beaten

2 cups milk

1 cup flour

2 teaspoons salt

1 teaspoon pepper

Serves 8.

Butter a 1½ to 2-quart casserole. Drain chiles, reserving liquid. Rinse chiles; remove seeds. Combine cheeses. Layer a third of the chiles and a third of the cheeses in casserole; repeat to make 3 layers. Combine remaining ingredients including reserved chiles liquid. Pour over chiles-cheese layers. Bake at 325° for 1 hour.

PASTA COUSTEAU

This will bring you rave notices.

1 cup whipping cream

3 ounces Gorgonzola cheese, crumbled

⅓ cup Ricotta cheese

3 tablespoons butter

Freshly ground pepper

1 ounce vodka

1 teaspoon Grand Marnier (optional)

1 (10-ounce) package frozen chopped spinach, thawed and well drained

1 pound linguine or fettucine

⅓ cup Parmesan cheese, freshly grated

Serves 4.

Heat cream over medium heat; add cheeses and butter, stirring until blended. Add pepper, vodka, Grand Marnier and spinach; heat through. Keep warm until ready to serve.

Cook pasta according to directions; drain and toss with sauce. Serve immediately with fresh Parmesan sprinkled on top.

VERMICELLI ALLA VONGOLE À LA ROBERTSON

1 cup celery, finely chopped

1 cup scallions, finely chopped

⅓ cup garlic, finely chopped

⅓ cup pecans or walnuts, finely chopped

Oil

Pepper

2 (10½-ounce) cans white clam sauce

3 tablespoons Chablis or dry white wine

1 (8.8-ounce) angel hair pasta

Serves 6 to 8.

Sauté chopped celery, scallions, garlic and nuts in oil approximately 5 to 8 minutes over low heat; season with pepper if desired. Add clam sauce (red clam sauce may be used if preferred) and wine. Continue cooking over low heat for 7 minutes. Pour over pasta of your choice (I prefer capelli di angeli, a fine spaghetti). Be prepared to serve seconds and thirds.

Cliff Robertson

Cliff Robertson

Star of stage, screen and television; Grand Marshall of the 1986 Rose Festival Grand Floral Parade, and the man who reaches out and touches us all.

WALNUT SPINACH LASAGNA

12 ounces lasagna pasta

1 tablespoon butter

1 tablespoon olive oil

7 cloves garlic, chopped

4 shallots, chopped

2 cups walnuts, chopped

2 (10-ounce) packages frozen chopped spinach, thawed

Dash cayenne

Generous grating of nutmeg

¼ cup butter or margarine

¼ cup flour

Spinach liquid plus milk to make 2 cups

1 tablespoon Parmesan cheese, grated

Salt and pepper to taste

3 eggs

2 cups Ricotta cheese

½ cup plus 1 tablespoon Parmesan cheese, grated

½ cup Romano cheese, grated

8 ounces Mozzarella, grated

Walnut halves for garnish

Serves 8 to 10.

Cook lasagna pasta in boiling, salted water until tender but still firm to the bite. Drain and rinse.

Sauté garlic and shallots in 1 tablespoon butter and oil. Add chopped walnuts; stir 1 minute. Squeeze moisture from thawed spinach; retain this liquid to mix with milk for cream sauce. Add drained spinach to garlic-walnut mixture; add cayenne and nutmeg. Remove from heat.

To make cream sauce, melt butter; add flour, stir for 1 minute. Add milk with spinach liquid and cook, stirring constantly, until thickened and bubbling. Add Parmesan, salt and pepper. Set aside.

Beat eggs; add Ricotta and beat until smooth. Add 1 tablespoon Parmesan, salt and pepper.

Combine remaining Parmesan, Romano and Mozzarella cheeses.

In a deep 9 x 13-inch baking pan, layer pasta, spinach-walnut mixture, cream sauce, Ricotta mixture and cheeses. Repeat. Garnish with walnut halves. Bake at 350° until hot and bubbling, about 45 minutes.

Robert and Sally Bailey

Robert and Sally Bailey

Gourmet cooks; he is Executive Director of the Portland Opera.

BAKED FLORENTINE CROISSANT

A crisp and flavorful filled croissant.

1 tablespoon oil

1 tablespoon butter

¼ cup onion, chopped

½ pound mushrooms, sliced

¼ cup dry white wine

1 (10-ounce) package frozen, chopped spinach, well drained

2 tablespoons parsley, chopped

½ teaspoon salt

Dash pepper

Cheese Sauce:

4 tablespoons butter

4 tablespoons flour

¾ teaspoon salt

Dash pepper

Freshly ground nutmeg

2 cups whole milk

⅓ cup Swiss cheese, grated

10 croissants

¾ pound Swiss cheese, sliced

Serves 10.

Melt oil and butter in saucepan (do not use aluminum). Add onion; cook 2 to 3 minutes. Add mushrooms; cook 5 minutes. Add wine and simmer to reduce liquid by half. Add spinach, parsley and seasonings; set aside.

To make cheese sauce, melt butter over medium heat; blend in flour and seasoning, stirring until mixture is smooth and bubbly. Add milk and cook until thickened; add grated cheese and stir until melted. Add spinach mixture to cheese sauce. Sauce can be made in advance and stored in refrigerator.

To assemble, split croissants in half lengthwise; place a slice of Swiss cheese on bottom half of each. Spoon filling over cheese slice, top with a second cheese slice and top of the croissant. Place croissants on cookie sheet and bake at 350° for 7 minutes or more, until warmed through and cheese melts.

Supporting

Cast

VEGETABLES & CONDIMENTS

ARTICHOKE CASSEROLE

A special and different flavor, yet simple to prepare.

3 tablespoons butter

2 tablespoons olive oil

1 package frozen artichokes, thawed

1 large tomato, peeled, seeded and chopped

½ clove garlic, minced

½ teaspoon dried basil

2 cups chicken bouillon

1 cup long grain rice

1 teaspoon salt

½ teaspoon pepper

Parsley, chopped

Freshly grated Parmesan cheese

Serves 4 to 6.

Heat 2 tablespoons of butter and the olive oil in a heavy sauce pan. Add artichokes. Cook, stirring constantly for 3 minutes. Add tomato, garlic, basil and ½ cup of the bouillon. Simmer, covered, over low heat until artichokes are half tender.

Heat remaining 1 tablespoon butter in 2-quart saucepan. Add rice and cook over medium heat, stirring constantly, until rice is yellow and transparent. Add remaining 1½ cups bouillon, salt and pepper. Simmer over lowest heat until rice is almost but not quite done.

Add artichoke mixture to rice and stir well. Simmer, covered until rice and artichokes are tender but still firm. If necessary, add a little more hot bouillon to prevent scorching. Transfer to a heated serving dish. Sprinkle with parsley and Parmesan cheese and serve.

SWISS GREEN BEANS

Doubles easily; a vegetable that can be prepared ahead.

1 (10-ounce) package frozen French green beans

1 tablespoon butter

1 tablespoon flour

½ teaspoon salt

⅛ teaspoon pepper

1 teaspoon sugar

1 teaspoon onion, grated

1 cup sour cream

¼ cup grated Swiss cheese

½ cup corn flakes, crushed

Serves 4.

Cook beans as directed; drain and place in casserole.

Melt butter in top of double boiler over simmering water. Stir in flour, salt, pepper, sugar, onion and sour cream. Cook, stirring until thick. While still hot, add Swiss cheese. Pour over green beans. Sprinkle corn flakes over top, dot with butter and bake at 350° for 20 minutes.

TIPSY BAKED BEANS

A different flavor and easy on the digestion.

3 strips bacon

½ green pepper, chopped

1 clove garlic, diced

¼ cup bourbon

1 (55-ounce) can B & M baked beans

2 teaspoons Dijon mustard

1 teaspoon catsup

2 teaspoons brown sugar

1 tablespoon molasses

Serves 4 to 6.

Cut bacon into small pieces; sauté over low heat. When fat has been released, add green pepper and garlic; sauté until pepper is soft and garlic is golden. Drain fat. Add bourbon and simmer until juices thicken. Add to beans along with remaining ingredients. Place in a covered casserole and bake at 350° for 30 minutes.

BROCCOLI STIR FRY

Wonderful with Stir Fry Chicken Cashew.

1½ teaspoons salt

8 slices ginger root, minced

2 tablespoons white wine

2 teaspoons sugar

2 to 3 tablespoons oil

2 pounds fresh broccoli, trimmed (use flowerets only)

Serves 4 to 6.

Mix salt, ginger, wine, and sugar, set aside.

Heat oil in wok for 20 to 30 seconds. Add broccoli and toss continuously 2 to 3 minutes.

Add sauce to broccoli; stir all together until broccoli is desired doneness, still somewhat crisp. Do not overcook.

COTTAGE BROCCOLI

1 bunch broccoli, trimmed into flowerets

2 eggs

1 cup cottage cheese

1 teaspoon onion, minced

½ teaspoon salt

¼ teaspoon pepper

1 teaspoon Worcestershire sauce

2 ounces Cheddar cheese, grated

¼ cup butter, melted

½ cup fresh bread crumbs

Serves 6 to 8.

Boil broccoli in uncovered pan until tender-crisp. Drain and arrange in a buttered casserole.

Combine eggs, cottage cheese, onion, salt, pepper, Worcestershire, cheese and half of the butter. Pour over broccoli.

Mix remaining butter with bread crumbs and sprinkle over the top. Bake at 350° for 30 minutes or until golden.

Can be made ahead and baked later; easily doubled.

BIG SUR MEDLEY

Three medium zucchini, sliced, or one package spinach may be substituted for the broccoli.

1 cup enriched long grain rice

1 large bunch broccoli, trimmed into flowerets

1 (7-ounce) can whole green chiles

12 ounces Monterey Jack cheese, grated

1 large tomato, thinly sliced

Salt and pepper

2 cups sour cream

1 teaspoon garlic salt

1 teaspoon crushed oregano

¼ green pepper, minced

¼ cup green onion, minced

2 tablespoons chopped parsley

Serves 6 to 8.

Cook rice according to package directions; set aside. Cook broccoli in lightly salted water just until tender-crisp; drain and set aside. Using a 3-quart well buttered casserole, place rice in an even layer at the bottom. Remove seeds from chiles and coarsely chop; sprinkle over rice. Top with half the cheese. Arrange broccoli over the cheese and top with thinly sliced tomato. Season with salt and pepper.

Gently combine sour cream with garlic salt, oregano, green pepper, green onion and parsley. Spoon this evenly over the layer of tomatoes; top with remaining cheese. Bake at 350° for approximately 45 minutes.

BRUSSELS SPROUTS WITH CIDER VINEGAR

You'll like these hot or cold.

2 cups fresh Brussels sprouts

¼ cup cider vinegar

Serves 4.

Wash and trim sprouts. Boil in generous amount of water just until cooked; they should still be bright green. Drain well and return to pan. Add vinegar and toss over heat for 1 to 2 minutes. Drain again. Serve immediately.

CARROTS JULIENNE

Beautiful and surprisingly crisp.

1½ pounds carrots

Boiling water

Ice water

4 tablespoons butter

¼ dry white wine

¼ cup sugar

½ teaspoon salt

½ white pepper

½ teaspoon marjoram

1½ teaspoons minced fresh parsley

½ cup slivered almonds

1 tablespoon butter

Serves 6.

Peel carrots and julienne. Add to boiling water; return to boil for l minute. Drain; plunge immediately into ice water; cool completely. Remove from ice water and pat dry. If done in advance, place carrots in refrigerator until ready to use.

Melt butter in frying pan. Add carrots and sauté about 2 minutes over moderately high heat, stirring to make sure they are well coated with butter. Add wine and reduce. Add sugar and cook about two minutes until liquid is gone. Add salt, pepper, marjoram and parsley. May set aside at this point and reheat before serving.

Sauté almonds in 1 tablespoon butter until golden. Sprinkle over carrots just before serving.

FRIED FRESH CARROTS

Carrots and garlic — a new combination.

8 medium carrots, sliced

4 tablespoons butter or margarine or enough to coat carrots

2 small cloves garlic or 1 clove fresh elephant garlic, crushed

Serves 4.

Heat butter in heavy skillet; add crushed garlic. Add carrots to butter, stirring constantly over medium high heat for 3 minutes. Lower heat slightly and stir occasionally until carrots are tender when tested with a fork.

Carrots should be slightly browned but not burned. Strain off extra butter and serve.

CORN CUSTARD

2½ cups fresh corn

½ cup Eaglebrand milk

½ cup green pepper, chopped

2 tablespoons pimento, chopped

1 tablespoon onion, chopped

1 teaspoon salt

2 eggs, well beaten

Serves 4.

Combine all ingredients in casserole. Bake at 350° for 1 hour. Frozen or canned corn may be substituted for fresh.

NUTTY EGGPLANT

A texture like stuffing plus the crunch of nuts; excellent with roast lamb or beef.

1 medium eggplant

2 slices buttered bread or ¾ cup coarse
   bread crumbs

1 egg, beaten

1 tablespoon dehydrated onion or 1½ tablespoons grated onion

½ teaspoon dry basil or marjoram

½ cup slivered almonds

Salt and pepper to taste

Serves 4.

Peel and cube eggplant. Cook in saucepan with ½ cup water, enough not to boil dry. Cook 5 minutes or until soft enough to mash; drain and mash. Add remaining ingredients. Pour into a buttered 1½-quart casserole; dot with butter

Bake at 350° for 30 minutes. May be frozen.

BAKED EGGPLANT SLICES

This crisp, cheese flavored eggplant may become a favorite.

1 cup mayonnaise or salad dressing

¼ cup milk

1 tablespoon lemon juice

¼ teaspoon salt

1 medium eggplant, unpeeled and cut into ½″ slices

3 cups rich cheese flavored crackers, finely crushed

Serves 4 to 6.

In a bowl combine mayonnaise, milk, lemon juice and salt.

Season eggplant slices with additional salt and pepper if desired. Dip each slice into mayonnaise mixture, then coat with crumbs. Place eggplant slices in an ungreased 15 x 10 x 1-inch baking dish. Bake at 350° for 25 to 30 minutes or until slices are crisp and hot.

MUSHROOMS MONTEREY

A favorite with grilled steaks or barbecued meats.

1 pound mushrooms, sliced

2 tablespoons butter

½ cup sour cream

¼ teaspoon salt

½ cup Parmesan cheese, freshly grated

¼ cup chopped parsley

Serves 4.

Sauté mushrooms in butter. Combine with remaining ingredients. Turn into a small casserole and bake 20 to 25 minutes at 350°.

MUSHROOM MARJORAM CASSEROLE

An excellent luncheon entrée with a fruit salad; may also be served as an accompaniment to meat.

½ teaspoon dried marjoram

1 tablespoon chives, chopped

1 pound mushrooms, cut in half

½ cup butter(1 cube), melted

½ cup chicken broth

¼ cup dry sherry

¼ teaspoon salt

¼ teaspoon pepper

Serves 4 to 6.

Combine all ingredients in greased, covered casserole. Bake at 350° for 15 to 20 minutes.

Serve at once on thin crisp toast points in individual ramekins.

WALLA WALLA ONION CASSEROLE

If Walla Walla sweets are not in season, try with yellow onions and a teaspoon of sugar.

4 tablespoons butter

5 cups Walla Walla onions, chopped

1 teaspoon salt

½ cup white rice, uncooked

2 cups boiling water

1 cup sour cream

1 cup Swiss or Cheddar cheese, grated

Serves 6.

Melt butter in large fry pan. Add onions and salt; sauté until soft but do not brown. Cook rice in boiling water 5 minutes. Drain and add to onions. Stir in sour cream.

In buttered 8 x 11-inch casserole layer onions alternately with cheese, ending with cheese layer. Bake at 350° for 30 minutes, covered, and an additional 15 minutes uncovered, or until brown.

BROILED STUFFED TOMATOES

A south of the border way to utilize those wonderful summer tomatoes.

2 large tomatoes

½ cup sour cream

1 tablespoon Jalapeño peppers, chopped

3 tablespoons green onions, sliced

2 teaspoons flour

¾ teaspoon sugar

½ teaspoon salt

¼ cup Monterey Jack cheese, grated

¼ cup Cheddar cheese, grated

Serves 4.

Cut tomatoes in half horizontally; if necessary, cut a thin slice off each uncut end so that tomatoes will not tilt. Gently remove seeds and juice of tomatoes; drain upside down on paper towels.

In small bowl, combine sour cream, peppers, onions, flour, sugar and salt; mix well. Place tomato halves upright on foil lined baking sheet. Spoon ¼ of the sour cream mixture into each tomato cup. Broil 2 to 3 minutes or until sour cream is bubbly and lightly browned. Sprinkle tomatoes with cheeses; broil 2 to 3 additional minutes until cheeses are melted. Garnish with additional Jalapeno peppers if desired. Green peppers can be substituted for Jalapeño peppers.

ZUCCHINI JACK

4 eggs, slightly beaten

½ cup milk

3 tablespoons flour

1 teaspoon salt

2 teaspoons baking powder

8 small zucchini, sliced

12 ounces Monterey Jack cheese, grated

l (4-ounce) can chopped green chiles, drained

1 clove garlic, mashed, or ¼ teaspoon garlic powder

¼ cup fresh parsley, chopped

2 tablespoons butter, melted

1 cup seasoned croutons

Serves 12.

Combine eggs and milk. Sift flour, baking powder and salt and beat into egg mixture. Stir in zucchini, cheese, chiles, garlic and parsley. Pour into a greased 9 x 13-inch baking pan.

Combine butter and croutons; sprinkle over zucchini mixture. Bake at 350° for 35 to 45 minutes, until set. Let casserole sit 10 minutes before serving.

SPINACH-FILLED BAKED POTATOES

Wrap individually, freeze and reheat as needed.

4 large Russet potatoes, baked, scooped out while hot and mashed

½ cup butter or margarine (1 cube)

1 to 1½ teaspoon salt

1 teaspoon sugar

1 teaspoon dill weed

¼ teaspoon white pepper

1 package frozen chopped spinach, thawed

¼ cup chopped chives or 2 to 3 green onions, finely chopped

2 to 4 tablespoons fresh parsley, chopped

Milk or cream

¼ cup grated Parmesan cheese or ½ cup grated Cheddar cheese

Serves 4.

Combine butter, salt, sugar, dill weed and pepper; beat into mashed potatoes.

Squeeze moisture out of spinach; add to potatoes with chives and parsley. Add milk if necessary for desired consistency; mixture should be fairly soft as there will be some drying during re-baking. Taste and correct seasoning.

Spoon potato mixture back into shells; can cover and chill or freeze at this point.

Bake at 350°, uncovered, 30 to 45 minutes or until very hot. Sprinkle cheese on top during last few minutes of baking.

POTATO CLOUDS

Can make ahead and reheat; perfect for a holiday dinner.

2½ cups mashed potatoes

1 cup small curd cottage cheese

½ cup sour cream

2 tablespoons green onions, chopped

Salt and pepper to taste

1 teaspoon dried parsley

2 teaspoons garlic salt

3 eggs yolks, slightly beaten

3 egg whites, slightly beaten

Serves 6.

Mix all ingredients except egg whites in large bowl; fold egg whites into mixture. Place in 2-quart buttered casserole and bake at 350° for 1 hour.

GRATIN DAUPHINOIS

Scalloped potatoes in garlic and cream.

2 pounds boiling potatoes

2 cups milk

1½ cups heavy cream

1 large or 2 small cloves garlic, finely chopped

¾ teaspoon salt

½ teaspoon freshly ground pepper

½ cup Swiss cheese, grated

Serves 8.

Wash and peel potatoes; dry thoroughly. Slice ⅛-inch thick. Place in large saucepan. Add milk, cream, garlic, salt and pepper and bring to a boil, stirring to prevent scorching.

Preheat oven to 400°. Remove pan from heat; pour potatoes into a shallow baking dish that has been heavily buttered. Sprinkle cheese over top. Bake 1 hour or until potatoes are done and well-browned; reduce heat to 375° if dish begins to brown too much on surface. Let stand 10 minutes before serving to allow sauce to thicken. Serve either hot or cold.

FOUR STAR POTATOES

2½ pounds red potatoes

1 tablespoon red wine vinegar

1 tablespoon Dijon mustard

½ cup olive oil

1½ teaspoons caraway seeds

¼ cup minced fresh parsley

3 tablespoons Bermuda onion, chopped

Salt and pepper

Serves 6.

Wash potatoes; slice ¼-inch thick. Steam over boiling water, about 8 to 10 minutes.

Heat vinegar, mustard and oil in a saucepan, using a whisk to blend. Add caraway seeds, parsley and onion. When all is warm toss lightly over hot potatoes. Add salt and pepper if desired.

SCALLOPED HASH BROWNS

Try with breakfast, lunch or dinner.

1 (2-pound) bag frozen hash brown potatoes, cubed or shredded

1 can cream of chicken soup

1 cup onion, chopped

1 pint sour cream

8 ounces sharp Cheddar cheese, grated

Salt and pepper to taste

Crushed corn flakes

½ cup butter or margarine (1 cube), melted

Paprika

Serves 10 to 12.

Mix potatoes, soup, onion, sour cream, cheese, salt and pepper. Pour into 9 x 13-inch baking pan. Top with crushed corn flakes well mixed with melted butter; sprinkle with paprika. Bake 1 hour at 350°.

ORIENTAL OVEN RICE

4 slices bacon, cubed

1 cup long grain rice

¼ teaspoon salt

2 ounces slivered almonds

1 medium onion, diced

4 tablespoons butter

1 (4-ounce) can mushrooms, drained

1 can Campbell's beef bouillon

1 can Campbell's beef consommé

1 soup can water

1½ tablespoons soy sauce

Serves 8 to 10.

In a frying pan, combine and brown the first 6 ingredients; cook for about 10 minutes. Place in a 1½-quart casserole.

Mix remaining ingredients and add to casserole. Bake uncovered at 300° for 3 hours.

Top will be quite brown as soy colors the rice.

WILD RICE AND MUSHROOM CASSEROLE

2 tablespoons butter

½ pound fresh mushrooms, sliced

½ cup wild rice

½ cup brown rice

2½ cups water

1 teaspoon salt

½ cup sour cream

4 sprigs parsley, chopped

Ground pepper

Serves 4 to 6.

In saucepan melt butter; add mushrooms and sauté until just soft. Add rices, water and salt; bring to a boil. Cover and simmer 50 minutes or until done. Stir in sour cream and parsley; season with pepper.

Jane Hibler

Cookbook author and food columnist for The Oregonian.

ARROZ CON CHILES

Add cooked chicken to this for a main dish casserole.

3 cups sour cream

2 (4-ounce) cans green chiles, chopped

4 cups cooked rice

Salt and pepper to taste

¾ pound Monterey Jack cheese, grated

4 ounces Cheddar cheese, grated

Serves 6 to 8.

Mix sour cream and chiles. Season rice with salt and pepper. In a buttered 3-quart casserole, layer rice, sour cream mixture and grated Monterey Jack, ending with rice. Sprinkle with grated Cheddar cheese. Bake 30 minutes at 350°.

BARLEY PILAF

Delicious with shish kekabs or lamb roast; include water chestnuts for added crunch.

2 medium onions, coarsely chopped

¾ pound mushrooms, sliced

½ cup butter or margarine (1 cube)

1¾ cups pearl barley

1 quart chicken or beef stock

Serves 12.

Preheat oven to 350°

Heat 2 tablespoons butter in large heavy skillet and cook mushrooms gently for 4 to 5 minutes. Lift out mushrooms; add remaining butter and cook onions until wilted. Pour in barley and cook slowly, turning frequently until it browns to the color of an almond. Add cooked mushrooms and 1¾ cups chicken stock. Cover tightly; bake 30 minutes. Remove lid, taste for seasoning and add another 1¾ cups stock. Bake 30 minutes longer adding more stock if needed. Bake 10 to 30 minutes longer depending upon how tender you like barley, but don't let it become mushy.

Can be baked half way the day before and finished the day of serving; freezes well.

SPAETZLE

The combination of milk and water and the resting period are old Swiss secrets contributing to the tenderness of these noodles.

½ cup milk

½ cup water

2 eggs

2 cups flour

Pinch salt

Boiling water

2 teaspoons salt

Optional:

Butter

Buttered crumbs

Grated cheese

Serves 6.

Beat first 5 ingredients together with a wire whisk, adding more flour if necessary to make batter the consistency of thick pancake dough. Let rest an hour. Add more flour or liquid if necessary to maintain proper consistency.

Fill an 8-quart kettle with boiling water; add salt. Push dough through a spaetzle sieve or a colander, or drop small bits from the tip of a spoon into the boiling water. Boil only a few minutes. Spaetzle will come to top of pan when done.

Remove pan from heat. Pour a small bowl of cold water into pan to prevent noodles from sticking.

Drain in colander. Place on heated platter and serve with melted butter or buttered crumbs, or a combination of buttered crumbs and grated cheese. If cheese is used, place platter in heated oven briefly to melt cheese. Serve at once.

POPPYSEED NOODLES

A big hit with our testers.

1 (10-ounce) package egg noodles

2 to 4 tablespoons butter or margarine

½ pint sour cream

1 pint cottage cheese

½ to 1 teaspoon cracked or lemon pepper

½ to 1 teaspoon salt or garlic salt

1 tablespoon or more poppy seeds

Parmesan cheese, grated (optional)

Chopped parsley, (optional)

Serves 4 to 6.

Cook and drain noodles.

Heat remaining ingredients except Parmesan and parsley; do not simmer or boil. When heated, add noodles and toss to coat with sauce; be sure mixture is hot. If desired, add Parmesan and parsley before serving.

CONDIMENTS

CUMBERLAND SAUCE

Fragrant and easy to make; gives a new flavor to chicken breasts.

10 ounces currant jelly

¼ cup orange juice

1 tablespoon lemon juice

¾ teaspoon powdered ginger

½ to 1 teaspoon grated orange rind

Serves 8 to 10.

Melt jelly; stir in remaining ingredients. Mix well and heat through, stirring until sauce is smooth.

Serve with lamb, game or poultry.

CUE: The true pleasure of cooking is sharing. There are many special recipes in this book which lend themselves to gift giving. The following condiments, many breads, cookies, candy and appetizer recipes would be applicable. Consider keeping quality and ease of packaging. These suggestions for presentation may stimulate your imagination: A brown paper bag is always on hand and can be elegant when tied with several strands of bright ribbons or raffia. Extra wine glasses, tumblers or mugs lend themselves as containers. A napkin or piece of fabric can be used as an interesting liner for a basket, tin or box. A terra cotta pot lined with foil can hold a variety of foods. Chilled fresh flowers or herbs are an attractive addition to a gift.

ZESTY BARBECUE SAUCE

1 (10-ounce) can condensed tomato soup

½ cup cider vinegar

½ cup brown sugar

1 tablespoon soy sauce

1 teaspoon celery seed

1 teaspoon salt

1 teaspoon chili powder

Dash cayenne pepper

2 tablespoons sweet or dill pickle relish (optional)

1 to 2 tablespoons onions, chopped (optional)

Makes approximately 2 cups.

Combine all ingredients and store in refrigerator.

Use in barbecued meat recipes such as spare ribs, pork chops, beef ribs; also good in meatloaf. Keeps well.

CHILI SAUCE

The aromas while cooking are wonderful. This has a sweet flavor.

6 quarts tomatoes, peeled and chopped

4 cups onions, chopped

4 cups green peppers, chopped

4 cups sugar

2⅔ cups white vinegar

2 tablespoons salt

2 tablespoons mustard seed

1 tablespoon celery seed

Dash paprika

1 teaspoon cinnamon

1 teaspoon nutmeg

1 teaspoon allspice

Makes 10 (12-ounce) jars.

Cook tomatoes slowly for 1 hour. Spoon off excess liquid; add peppers and onions. Cook until thick, stirring occasionally. Add remaining ingredients and continue cooking, stirring often, until thick.

Spoon into sterilized jars and seal.

Serve as an accompaniment to meat.

DILLED SOUR CREAM

Good on any kind of fish, especially fresh Northwest Chinook salmon, cooked on a grill with lemon and onion slices. Also good as a sauce for vegetables.

1 cup sour cream

1 teaspoon dill weed

1 tablespoon wine vinegar

¼ teaspoon sugar

1 teaspoon salt

2 teaspoons lemon juice (optional)

Makes 1 cup.

Mix ingredients and chill for at least 1 hour to blend flavors.

BABY ALICE'S MUSTARD

A sweet and hot mustard.

1 tablespoon flour

5 tablespoons dry mustard

½ teaspoon salt

½ cup sugar

Dash cayenne pepper

2 eggs

½ cup white vinegar

4 tablespoons butter

Makes 1½ to 2 cups.

Combine dry ingredients in a small bowl. Beat eggs in top of double boiler; add dry ingredients and vinegar. Cook over hot water, stirring constantly, until thick and smooth. Remove from heat, add butter cut in chunks; stir to melt. Spoon into jar.

This superb mustard keeps for months in the refrigerator, and is excellent with ham, poultry and cold poached salmon. Recipe is easily doubled.

CREAMY MUSTARD SAUCE FOR HAM

2 tablespoons dry mustard

¼ teaspoon salt

1 tablespoon sugar

2 tablespoons cider vinegar

1 tablespoon water

1 beaten egg

½ cup whipping cream, whipped

Makes 1½ cups.

Combine first 5 ingredients; mix well. Add beaten egg and heat in double boiler, stirring until thick. Cool; fold in whipped cream. Keeps well in refrigerator.

MARINATED MUSHROOMS

Even better the second day. May be used as a relish or side dish. Try on crackers for an appetizer.

1 pound fresh mushrooms, cleaned and sliced

2 cups water

2 teaspoons parsley, chopped

¼ teaspoon salt

½ teaspoon pepper

½ teaspoon oregano

¼ teaspoon basil

2 tablespoons grated onion and juice

1 clove garlic, minced

⅓ cup pimento-stuffed olives, sliced or chopped

1 teaspoon sugar

¼ cup oil

¼ cup wine vinegar

Serves 8.

Simmer sliced mushrooms in water 3 to 5 minutes; drain; arrange in shallow dish. Combine remaining ingredients and pour over mushrooms. Refrigerate, stirring occasionally, for 12 hours or longer.

DILLED CARROTS

Serve as a low-sugar snack or relish.

2 cups carrots, sliced or cut in thin sticks

½ yellow onion, thinly sliced

1 large clove garlic, sliced

1 teaspoon dill weed or dill seed

½ cup vinegar

½ cup water

1 teaspoon salt

½ teaspoon sugar

Makes 4 cups.

Combine carrots, onion, garlic and dill in glass jar or bowl.

Combine vinegar, water, salt and sugar in small saucepan. Bring to a boil and pour over carrots.

Cover; refrigerate for 24 hours. Drain and serve.

TENNESSEE TOMATO RELISH

The contributor of this recipe wrote, "This is my grandmother's recipe. Everything was fresh from the garden, and she never measured anything. Amounts are approximate, so vary to suit your taste. Good with any meat or poultry."

2 large tomatoes, chopped

1 large sweet green pepper, chopped

3 to 4 green onions, chopped

¼ cup cider vinegar

2 tablespoons sugar

1 teaspoon salt, or to taste

Black pepper to taste

Makes 4 cups.

Combine all ingredients and chill. Keeps well for several days if refrigerated.

CURRIED FRUIT

A condiment that goes with beef, pork, lamb and poultry.

½ cup butter (1 cube)

1 to 2 teaspoons curry powder

½ cup brown sugar

1 (28-ounce) can sliced peaches, drained

1 (20-ounce) can pineapple chunks, drained

1 (28-ounce) can pears, drained and sliced

Maraschino cherries, a few for color

2 bananas, sliced (optional)

Serves 10 to 12.

Prepare a day ahead.

Preheat oven to 350°. Melt butter with curry and brown sugar. Arrange well-drained fruit in casserole; pour butter mixture over all. Cover and bake for 1 hour.

Refrigerate overnight and reheat to serve.

CRANBERRY CONSERVE

A refreshing replacement for cranberry sauce that makes an excellent hostess gift during the holidays.

2 cups water

2 cups sugar

1 pound cranberries, washed

Grated rind of one orange

½ cup broken walnuts

2 teaspoons crystallized ginger, slivered

Makes 4 cups.

Stir water and sugar in saucepan until sugar is dissolved. Boil 5 minutes; add cranberries. Simmer uncovered, without stirring, until skins pop and consistency is clear and thick, 3 to 5 minutes. Add orange rind, nuts and ginger. Pour into a jar and chill.

CRISP AND SWEET ZUCCHINI PICKLES

1 gallon zucchini, peeled, seeded and cut into 1-inch cubes (use a fluted fruit cutter if possible)

1 gallon cold water

1 cup hydrated lime (horticultural lime can be purchased at garden supply store)

24 cups sugar

13½ cups apple cider vinegar

5¼ tablespoons plain salt (not iodized)

4½ tablespoons whole cloves

9 to 12 sticks cinnamon broken in small pieces

Makes 9 to 10 pints.

Do not use aluminum container or utensil for any of this preparation.

Place zucchini, water and lime in large stainless steel or enamel container. Let stand for 24 hours, stirring often with wooden spoon. After 24 hours, rinse well. Soak in clear water for 3 hours. Rinse and drain.

Mix remaining ingredients in large kettle and heat until dissolved; cool. Add zucchini and let stand for 24 hours. After 24 hours bring syrup and zucchini to a boil; boil for 35 minutes, stirring often.

Fill hot sterilized jars with zucchini and syrup, distributing the spices as evenly as possible. Seal jars. Pickles will be ready in about one month.

PERFECT DILL PICKLES

This recipe has less salt than most pickle recipes. The pickles resemble German gherkins.

1 cup white vinegar

4 cups water

¼ cup rock salt

Fresh dill sprigs

Garlic cloves

Small or medium size fresh pickling cucumbers

Combine first three ingredients. Simmer 5 minutes. Adjust amount of brine according to the number of cucumbers you are processing.

Place cucumbers in sterilized jars with generous sprig of dill and one garlic clove. Fill with vinegar brine. Seal. Process in hot water bath 5 minutes in canning kettle. Pickles are ready to eat in 7 days.

Intermissions

S A L A D S

LeTOURNEAU'S SALAD

Marinated mushrooms make the dressing for this salad distinctive.

4 tablespoons red or white wine vinegar

⅔ cup cooking oil

Ground pepper

½ teaspoon salt

Parsley flakes

2 garlic cloves, minced

1 cup fresh mushrooms, sliced

Leaf lettuce

1 avocado,cubed

1 Spanish onion, sliced

1 green pepper, cubed

Serves 6.

Make marinade of wine vinegar, oil, pepper, salt, parsley flakes and minced garlic. Pour over mushrooms and marinate overnight in refrigerator, covered. Shake well before using.

Toss lettuce, avocado, onion and green pepper. Add marinated undrained mushrooms just before serving.

GREEN SALAD WITH OREGON BLUE AND WALNUTS

Salad greens for 4, well chilled

4 ounces walnuts, chopped

4 ounces Oregon blue cheese, crumbled

½ red pepper, sliced

½ red onion, sliced

¼ cup Old Monk olive oil

¼ cup Saffola oil

3 to 4 tablespoons red wine vinegar

Salt and pepper to taste

Serves 4.

Place greens, walnuts, cheese, red pepper and onion in a salad bowl. Mix the remaining ingredients together and pour over the greens.
Toss and serve immediately.

Jane Hibler

Jane Hibler

Cookbook author and food columnist for The Oregonian.

WATERCRESS SALAD

The dressing is a marvelous complement to the sharp zing of watercress.

1 pound watercress, stems removed

6 eggs, hard-cooked and finely chopped

½ pound bacon, cooked and finely chopped

⅓ cup vinegar

1 cup corn oil

½ cup sugar

1 large onion, chopped

1 teaspoon Worcestershire sauce

1 teaspoon salt

Serves 4.

Gently toss watercress, eggs and bacon.

In a blender, combine remaining ingredients until creamy and smooth. Pour over watercress mixture just before serving

SKILLET SALAD

A wilted lettuce salad like grandmother used to make

4 slices bacon

¼ cup white vinegar

2 tablespoons water

2 tablespoons sugar

½ teaspoon salt

Lettuce of your choice, or torn spinach

Dash pepper

Hard-cooked egg, finely diced (optional)

Green onions, minced (optional)

Avocado, diced (optional)

Serves 4.

Fry bacon until crisp, Remove from skillet; drain on paper towels

Combine vinegar, water, sugar and salt with bacon fat in skillet; heat to boiling. Cool slightly. Pour over lettuce. Add crumbled bacon, pepper and any of the optional garnishes. Toss and serve immediately

SPINACH SALAD WITH MOZZARELLA

2 bunches spinach

6 slices bacon

4 green onions, sliced

½ pound fresh mushrooms, sliced

¼ cup Mozzarella cheese, grated

1 teaspoon sugar

¼ teaspoon paprika

½ teaspoon prepared mustard

3 tablespoons white wine vinegar

½ teaspoon salt

½ cup salad oil

½ teaspoon garlic salt

Dash freshly ground pepper

Serves 6 to 8.

Wash spinach, remove stems, drain and pat dry; chill.

Fry bacon until crisp; drain and crumble. Toss spinach, bacon, onions, mushrooms and cheese.

Mix remaining ingredients well. Pour over spinach mixture and toss lightly. Serve immediately.

NUTTY SPINACH SALAD

A very unusual spinach salad with a hint of the Far East.

2 tablespoons white wine vinegar with tarragon

1 tablespoon vermouth

2 teaspoons Dijon mustard

1 teaspoon soy sauce

½ teaspoon curry

½ teaspoon sugar

½ teaspoon salt

¼ teaspoon pepper

⅓ cup salad oil

2 bunches spinach leaves, washed, dried and torn

2 tablespoons sesame seeds, toasted

⅓ cup Spanish peanuts

1 or 2 green apples, cored and chopped

½ cup golden raisins

½ bunch green onions, chopped

Serves 6 to 8.

Mix first nine ingredients in bottom of large salad bowl. Add spinach; toss. Add remaining ingredients; toss again. Serve immediately.

Variations: Add 2 whole chicken breasts, cut in bite size pieces and sauteed in 2 tablespoons vegetable oil and 2 tablespoons soy sauce

MUSHROOM ORANGE SALAD

Pleasant in combination with poultry.

2 heads butter lettuce or 1 large head green leaf lettuce

1 can Mandarin oranges, drained

4 slices bacon

6 tablespoons salad oil

2 tablespoons white wine vinegar

3 tablespoons crumbled blue cheese

½ teaspoon salt

½ teaspoon dry mustard

⅛ teaspoon ground pepper

¼ cup slivered almonds, toasted

½ pound mushrooms, sliced

Serves 6 to 8.

Tear lettuce into bite-size pieces. Combine lettuce and oranges; refrigerate.

Cook bacon until crisp; drain and crumble. Set aside.

Combine remaining ingredients except mushrooms and almonds. Cover and chill.

To serve, pour dressing over chilled lettuce and oranges. Add bacon, almonds and mushrooms. Toss; serve immediately.

GRANNY JOANNE'S ROQUEFORT DRESSING

Makes a lot and keeps well in the refrigerator.

6 ounces Roquefort cheese, crumbled

1½ tablespoons Worcestershire sauce

Dash Tabasco

½ teaspoon garlic powder

½ teaspoon salt

1 pint mayonnaise

1 pint sour cream

Makes 4 cups.

Combine all ingredients; blend well. Chill.

ENSALADA NARANJA

Make this south of the border salad for any occasion.

1 or 2 heads romaine lettuce, shredded

2 or 3 oranges, peeled and sliced crosswise

1 cucumber, thinly sliced

1 red onion, sliced in thin rings

1 green pepper, diced

½ cup jicama, peeled and diced

¼ pound Jack cheese, cut in strips

2 ripe avocados, sliced and sprinkled with lemon juice and garlic powder

½ cup salad or olive oil

⅓ cup red wine vinegar

¼ teaspoon salt

¼ teaspoon celery seed

¼ cup ripe olives, pitted and sliced

Serves 8 to 10.

Place shredded romaine in salad bowl. Arrange oranges, vegetables, cheese and avocados on greens.

Combine oil, vinegar, salt and celery seed. Pour dressing over salad and mix lightly. Garnish with black olives.

SUNDAY'S SALAD DRESSING

A ranch dressing from scratch

1 small onion

1 clove garlic

3 cups sour cream

5 cups mayonnaise

2 teaspoons Lawry's seasoned salt

½ teaspoon white pepper

3 tablespoons dill weed

3 tablespoons parsley

Juice of 2 lemons

3 dashes Tabasco sauce

Makes 2 quarts.

Mince the onion and garlic. In large bowl, combine all ingredients; mix for 10 to 15 seconds at medium speed until light and airy. Refrigerate for 2 hours to meld flavors. Can be kept in refrigerator for a week. May also be used as a dip for fresh vegetables, chips or crackers.

COLD ASPARAGUS WITH PROSCIUTTO

An elegant first course.

16 large stalks asparagus

6 thin slices Prosciutto ham

1 egg

¼ cup olive oil

1 tablespoon Dijon mustard

Juice of ½ lemon

Salt and pepper to taste

2 tablespoons Parmesan cheese, grated

¼ teaspoon dill

Serves 4.

Wash and trim asparagus. Steam for 3 minutes, plunge into cold water, drain, then dry and chill.

Wrap center of asparagus with Prosciutto.

Beat egg, blend in oil; add Dijon mustard, lemon juice, salt and pepper.

Spoon a small amount of dressing over each serving. Sprinkle with Parmesan cheese and dill.

COLD BROCCOLI SALAD

Colorful and appealing to the eye.

Broccoli for 4 servings

½ cup olive oil

¼ cup tarragon white wine vinegar or lemon juice

1 clove garlic, mashed

1 teaspoon Dijon mustard

Salt and pepper to taste

½ cup toasted slivered almonds

Serves 4.

Blanch broccoli in large kettle of boiling salted water less than 5 minutes. Drain. Cover with ice water and chill ½ to 3 hours.

Combine remaining ingredients except almonds. Just before serving, drain broccoli well and pat dry. Drizzle dressing on individual servings and top with almonds.

MARINATED BROCCOLI SALAD

Great color, good texture.

1 package dry Good Seasons Italian dressing mix

1 tablespoon Worcestershire sauce

1 tablespoon soy sauce

2 pounds fresh broccoli, stems peeled, cut in bite-size pieces

¼ pound fresh mushrooms, sliced

1 green onion, sliced

1 clove garlic, crushed

¼ pound Cheddar cheese, cut in small cubes

1 avocado, sliced

1 fresh tomato, cubed

Makes 14 cups.

Follow package directions for making Italian dressing, adding Worcestershire and soy sauces.

Combine broccoli, mushrooms, onion, garlic and cheese in serving bowl. Pour half the dressing over the vegetables; refrigerate several hours.

Just before serving, add avocado, tomato and remaining dressing.

BEETS ZHIVAGO

Cool and refreshing, a delightful addition to a cold salad buffet.

1 (I6-ounce) can pickled beets

⅓ cup sour cream

1 tablespoon minced onion

1 teaspoon fresh lemon juice

Serves 8 to 10.

Drain beets and cut in julienne. Mix with other ingredients. Refrigerate 1 or 2 hours.

Serve in butter lettuce cups or as a cold side dish.

CONFETTI CABBAGE

Not a cole slaw; stays crisp for days.

4 cups finely shredded cabbage

½ green pepper, diced

½ red pepper, diced

1 onion, grated

1 cup sugar

½ cup salad oil

1 cup vinegar

½ cup water

½ teaspoon salt

Serves 6 to 8.

Combine ingredients and let stand overnight. Drain before serving.

If red peppers are not available, use a little pimento.

ROQUEFORT ONIONS

This will become a favorite; serve with sliced tomatoes and barbecued meats.

4 to 5 cups red onions, very thinly sliced

Hot water

1 cup Roquefort cheese, crumbled

½ cup olive oil

Juice of 1 lemon

¼ teaspoon black pepper

¼ teaspoon paprika

Serves 4 to 6.

Place sliced onions in a large bowl; cover with hot water for 2 minutes. Drain immediately.

Place remaining ingredients in a large jar; shake well. Pour dressing over drained onions. Marinate in refrigerator for 2 hours.

CRUNCHY TOMATO ASPIC

A favorite of Oswego Garden Club members.

2 tablespoons unflavored gelatin

4 cups tomato juice

1 teaspoon salt

3 tablespoons lemon juice

1 teaspoon Worcestershire sauce

1 cup chopped celery

½ cup sliced green onions

Shrimp (optional)

Chopped parsley (optional)

Stuffed green olives, sliced (optional)

Serves 6.

Soften gelatin in ½ cup cold tomato juice. Bring remaining tomato juice to a boil; add salt and softened gelatin. Simmer until gelatin is melted; remove from heat; add lemon juice and Worcestershire; chill. When aspic is about to set, add celery, onion, and any of the optional ingredients desired. Refrigerate until set.

NEW POTATO SALAD

½ pound fresh green beans

2 pounds small new red potatoes

¼ cup white wine vinegar

½ cup olive oil

1 large cucumber, peeled and sliced thinly

½ medium red onion, peeled and sliced thinly

2 tomatoes, sliced

2 teaspoons oregano

1 teaspoon basil

1 teaspoon salt, or to taste

Pepper to taste

Serves 6 to 8.

Clean green beans; cook in boiling, salted water until tender-crisp; drain. Plunge in ice water to stop cooking; drain again.

Scrub potatoes; cook until tender. Peel or leave skins on, as desired. Slice while warm and toss with combined vinegar and oil. Add remaining ingredients; refrigerate. Make several hours ahead to allow flavors to blend.

HOT GERMAN POTATO SALAD

4 to 6 slices bacon, minced

3 cups potatoes, cooked, peeled, sliced or diced

¼ to ½ cup onion, finely chopped

1 tablespoon flour

1 teaspoon salt

1 tablespoon sugar

¼ teaspoon dry mustard

⅓ cup vinegar

⅓ cup water

2 tablespoons sweet pickle relish (optional)

⅓ cup celery, thinly sliced (optional)

2 tablespoons green pepper, chopped (optional)

Serves 4 to 6.

Fry bacon until crisp; remove with slotted spoon; set aside. Sauté onion in about 3 table-spoons of the bacon fat until tender but not brown. Stir in flour, salt, sugar, and mustard. Add vinegar and water; cook until thickened, stirring constantly. Add potatoes, bacon, and any optional ingredients. Cover and heat slowly over very low heat for about 15 minutes; or pile in a casserole and heat in 350° oven 15 to 20 minutes. Can be made a day or more ahead, refrigerated in the casserole, and baked when ready to serve. Easily doubled or tripled.

GREEN PASTA SALAD

The cookbook committee requested this recipe; it's not "just another pasta salad."

½ cup fresh parsley, chopped

¾ cup fresh spinach leaves, chopped

1 clove garlic, mashed

4 green onions, sliced

2 rounded tablespoons pesto sauce or 3 tablespoons fresh basil or 1½ teaspoons dried basil

2 tablespoons fresh chives, minced

¾ cup Best Foods mayonnaise

¾ cup plain yogurt

Salt and pepper to taste

12 ounces small corkscrew noodles

6 quarts boiling water

2 tablespoons olive oil

1 clove garlic, mashed

1 tablespoon salt

Olive oil

Frozen peas, thawed (optional)

Shrimp meat (optional)

Salami (optional)

Pimentos (optional)

Serves 8 to 10.

In a blender or food processor, chop spinach, parsley, garlic and onions; add pesto or basil, chives, mayonnaise, yogurt, salt and pepper. Blend thoroughly and chill.

Add olive oil, garlic and salt to boiling water in large saucepot. Slowly add noodles and cook until tender, about 6 to 12 minutes. Drain well; transfer to bowl. Drizzle a little oil over noodles; sprinkle lightly with salt and pepper. Cool about 15 minutes, stirring occasionally. Add dressing and mix well. Add any desired optional ingredients. Chill thoroughly.

BOYSENBERRY SALAD

6 ounces raspberry gelatin

1 cup boiling water

1 cup pineapple juice

½ cup sweet wine (I use a Tokay)

1 can boysenberries, drained

1 cup crushed pineapple

½ cup chopped nut meats

Serves 6 to 8.

Dissolve gelatin in hot water; add pineapple juice and wine. Drain juice off boysenberries and measure out 1 cup of berries. Add to gelatin mixture along with remaining ingredients; mix well and pour into a ring mold; chill.

Alyce Rogers

Alyce Rogers
Well-known star of Portland opera.

BROWNELL'S ORANGE SALAD MOLD

This recipe is from a well-known holly growing pioneer family and is rich in orange flavor. When holly is in season, use it as a garnish.

2 (3-ounce) packages lemon gelatin

1 cup boiling water

1 (12-ounce) can frozen orange juice concentrate, undiluted

1 tablespoon lemon juice

2 cans mandarin oranges, drained, juice reserved

1 cup juice drained from mandarin oranges and crushed pineapple

1 cup crushed pineapple, drained, juice reserved

1 banana, mashed

2 tablespoons mayonnaise

1 cup heavy cream, whipped

Serves 8.

Dissolve gelatin in boiling water. Add juices, stirring until orange juice has melted. Stir in mandarin oranges; pour into a ring mold; refrigerate until set.

When ready to serve, combine remaining ingredients. Unmold salad; serve with dressing in center of ring.

OVERNIGHT FRUIT SALAD

A family tradition for holiday dinners for three generations.

4 egg yolks, beaten

Juice of 1 lemon

¼ cup heavy cream, unwhipped

1 cup heavy cream, whipped

1 (20-ounce) can pineapple chunks, drained

1 to 2 cups miniature marshmallows

1 cup walnuts, chopped

1 cup sliced bananas

1 cup canned pears, drained and cut into bite-size pieces

1 cup canned Royal Anne cherries, drained

Serves 10 to 12.

Combine egg yolks, lemon juice and ¼ cup cream in top of double boiler. Cook over hot water, stirring, until thickened. Cool.

Fold in whipped cream, pineapple and marshmallows; refrigerate overnight. When ready to serve, gently fold in remaining ingredients.

FROZEN FRUIT COMPOTE

Wonderful with brunch.

12 ounces frozen orange juice, undiluted

12 ounces water

2 cups sugar

1 tablespoon lemon juice

1 (16-ounce) can crushed pineapple, undrained

1 (16-ounce) can apricot halves, undrained

1 (16-ounce) can peaches, cut in bite-size pieces, undrained

4 bananas, sliced

Serves 10 to 12.

Gently combine all ingredients in large container; freeze. Take from freezer at least 3 hours before serving; consistency should be slushy. Spoon into small bowls for serving.

CITRUS SALAD DRESSING

A fruit salad dressing which refreshes the palate. Try over ice cream too.

1 egg, well beaten

1 cup sugar

Juice and grated rind of 1 lemon

Juice and grated rind of 1 orange

Juice and grated rind of 1 lime

Makes 1½ cups.

Combine all ingredients. Cook over medium heat, stirring constantly, until mixture comes to a boil; boil 1 minute. Cool, then refrigerate. Keeps well.

POPPY SEED DRESSING

Wonderful on grapefruit or fruit salad.

1 cup sugar

2 teaspoons dry mustard

2 teaspoons salt

⅔ cup white vinegar

¼ cup white onion, chopped

2 cups vegetable oil

3 tablespoons poppy seeds

Makes 3½ cups.

Mix sugar, mustard, salt, vinegar and chopped onion in food processor or blender. With machine running, slowly add oil; blend until thick. Add poppy seeds and blend thoroughly.

This makes a thick dressing that keeps a long time in the refrigerator.

SALMON SALAD AT ITS BEST

A molded seafood salad with elegant garnishes.

1 teaspoon dry mustard

½ teaspoon salt

1½ teaspoons sugar

2 egg yolks, slightly beaten

1½ tablespoons butter, melted

¾ cup milk

¼ cup white wine vinegar

1 tablespoon unflavored gelatin

2 tablespoons cold water

2 teaspoons lemon juice

1 teaspoon Worcestershire sauce

1 teaspoon onion, grated

½ to 1 cup celery, minced

1 pound fresh Chinook salmon, poached, boned and flaked, or 1 (1-pound) can Alaskan Sockeye salmon, boned and flaked

½ cup sour cream

½ cup mayonnaise

Lemon juice to taste

Dill weed to taste

6 fresh mushrooms, sliced

½ cup crème fraîche

1 tablespoon stone ground mustard

½ cucumber, thinly sliced

Rice wine vinegar

½ green olives stuffed with pimento

Serves 6.

In top of double boiler combine mustard, salt and sugar. Add egg yolks, butter, milk and vinegar. Cook over simmering water, stirring constantly, until somewhat thickened.

Soften gelatin in water and add to cooked mixture. Remove from heat; add lemon juice, Worcestershire and onion; cool.

When cool, fold in celery and salmon. Pour into Pam-sprayed mold or individual molds. Refrigerate until set.

For dressing, mix sour cream and mayonnaise. Add a generous amount of lemon juice and dill weed to taste.

For garnishes, mix mushrooms with crème fraîche and mustard. Marinate cucumber slices in rice vinegar to cover, for 3 hours.

When ready to serve unmold on a platter or on individual plates lined with butter lettuce and a few spinach leaves. Garnish with mushrooms, cucumbers and green olives. Serve dressing on the side or spoon over salad.

CRÈME FRAÎCHE

1 cup heavy cream

1 tablespoon buttermilk

Makes 1 cup.

Combine cream and buttermilk in a jar. Cover tightly and shake for at least 1 minute. Let stand at room temperature at least 8 hours or until thickened, then refrigerate. It will keep for 4 to 6 weeks.

May be used in place of sour cream in recipes or as a topping.

SHRIMP AND CRAB SALAD

The bread disappears into the body of the salad. Try also as a filling for cherry tomatoes or small cream puffs for the hors d'oeuvres table.

1 large loaf sliced sandwich bread

Softened butter

1 large onion, minced

6 hard-cooked eggs, diced

½ pound shrimp meat

1 pound crab meat

1 cup celery, finely cubed

3 cups mayonnaise

Juice of ½ lemon

Salt if desired

Serves 12.

Remove crusts from bread. Butter each slice lightly, then cube (about 20 cubes per slice). Add onion and eggs; cover and refrigerate overnight.

Combine mayonnaise and lemon juice. Fold into bread mixture with seafood and celery. Add salt if desired. Refrigerate 3 or 4 hours or overnight. Serve in lettuce cups, garnished as desired, or use as a filling for tomatoes or avocados. If crab is unavailable, use 1½ pounds shrimp.

ARTICHOKE AND SHRIMP SALAD

An excellent luncheon salad best made a day before serving.

1 box chicken-flavored Rice-a-Roni

2 (6-ounce) jars marinated artichoke hearts, drained, with liquid reserved, chopped

½ green pepper, chopped

½ cup pimento-stuffed green olives, sliced

4 green onions, chopped

8 ounces shrimp meat

½ cup mayonnaise

½ teaspoon curry powder

Serves 4 to 6.

Cook rice according to package directions, but omit butter. Cool, fluffing occasionally with a fork to prevent clumping together.

When cool, add vegetables and shrimp. Blend mayonnaise, curry and oil from artichokes and stir into salad.

CHICKEN SALAD LU CHOW

The toasted walnuts, olives and sautéed mushrooms are a taste treat.

4 cups chicken, cooked and coarsely chopped

½ cup mushrooms, sliced and sautéed in butter

5 to 6 green onions including tops, chopped

1 cup celery, chopped

1 cup green olives, sliced

1 cup ripe olives, sliced

1 cup walnut halves, toasted

1 cup Best Foods mayonnaise

1 cup heavy cream, whipped

Serves 12.

Combine all ingredients except whipped cream; chill thoroughly. Just before serving, fold in whipped cream. Serve on greens, garnished with tomatoes or with curried fruit as a condiment.

CHINESE CHICKEN SALAD

Demonstrated by Margie on "Two at Four".

½ pound chicken breasts

½ cup soy sauce

½ cup sugar

4 green onions, chopped

2 tablespoons almonds, chopped

2 tablespoons sesame seeds, toasted

2 ounces wonton wrappers

2 ounces or more mei-fun (rice stick)

Oil for frying

1 head iceberg lettuce, torn into bite-size pieces

2 tablespoons sugar

1 teaspoon salt

½ teaspoon pepper

¼ cup salad oil

1 teaspoon sesame oil

3 tablespoons white vinegar

Serves 4.

Skin and bone chicken. Chop into small pieces and place in soy sauce-sugar mixture. Bake in 375° oven one hour. Cool. Mix chicken in a large bowl along with the chopped green onions, almonds, toasted sesame seeds. Cut the wonton wrappers in strips and fry in hot oil until brown. Drop mei-fun in hot oil (be ready to take it out quickly, as it cooks in just a few seconds.) Add wonton, mei-fun and torn lettuce to bowl. Top with dressing made from remaining ingredients.

Richard Ross   Margie Boulé

Richard Ross and Margie Boulé

Richard is the dean of Portland TV anchormen and honorary board member of Lakewood Center. Margie is a favorite Portland television hostess. She has appeared in many local theater productions.

Grand

Finales

D E S S E R T S

OREGON HAZELNUT CHEESECAKE

Flavor is enhanced when made a day ahead.

2 pounds cream cheese, room temperature

1¾ cups sugar

4 eggs

½ teaspoon lemon rind, grated

1 cup hazelnuts, blanched and ground

Serves 10 to 12.

Beat cream cheese until smooth. Beat in sugar; add eggs, one at a time, only until blended. Fold in lemon rind and ground hazelnuts. Turn batter into 8 x 3-inch springform pan. Fill a larger pan with hot water to depth of 1½ inches when springform pan is placed inside. Bake at 350° for 1½ hours. Top should be golden brown and dry to touch.

Completely cool on rack. Invert on plate and refrigerate. Decorate with whole or chopped hazelnuts.

CHOCOLATE KAHLUA MOUSSE

Goes together in a matter of minutes and sets quickly; ideal for a busy cook with unexpected guests.

6 ounces semi-sweet chocolate

2 tablespoons Kahlua

2 tablespoons orange juice

2 egg yolks

2 eggs

1 teaspoon vanilla

3 to 4 tablespoons sugar

1 cup whipping cream

Serves 6.

Melt chocolate, Kahlua and orange juice in double boiler. With electric mixer, beat eggs, vanilla and sugar about 1½ minutes at medium speed. Add cream; blend about 30 seconds. Add chocolate mixture and blend until smooth. Divide among 6 individual serving dishes; refrigerate. If desired, serve with a dollop of whipped cream.

FLOATING ISLAND WITH CRÈME ANGLAISE

An elegant presentation; garnish with fresh fruit or flowers in season.

4 egg whites, room temperature

¼ teaspoon cream of tartar

¼ teaspoon salt

¾ cup fine granulated sugar

1 teaspoon vanilla

Dash nutmeg

Serves 4.

Beat egg whites until foamy; add cream of tartar and salt; continue to beat until soft peaks form. Add sugar 1 tablespoon at a time, continuing to beat. Add vanilla and nutmeg; beat 5 minutes. Fill 9 x 13-inch baking pans ⅓ to ½ full with boiling water. Spoon about 8 large mounds of meringue into the boiling water; do not crowd. Bake in preheated 400° oven about 5 minutes or until lightly browned. Remove with slotted spoon onto racks to drain. Place on platter or cookie sheet; refrigerate.

To serve, place meringues in individual shallow bowls or a punch bowl. Ladle Crème Anglaise over meringues. Recipe may be doubled.

CRÈME ANGLAISE

1½ cups milk

4 egg yolks

Dash ground mace

¼ cup sugar

⅛ to ¼ teaspoon salt

1 teaspoon vanilla

Dash ground nutmeg

Makes 2 cups.

Scald milk in top of double boiler; avoid forming skin. Beat egg yolks, mace, sugar and salt. Gradually stir milk into egg mixture. Return to double boiler; cook, stirring constantly until custard coats a metal spoon. Do not overcook or mixture will curdle. Cool quickly by placing pan in ice water. Stir in vanilla and nutmeg. Place a cover of plastic wrap directly on top of custard to avoid forming skin.

Recipe may be doubled. It is wonderful with Floating Islands or with fresh fruits or puddings.

LEMON SNOW PUDDING WITH RASPBERRY SAUCE

An elegant dessert that is refreshing and light.

1 envelope unflavored gelatin

¼ cup cold water

1 cup boiling water

¼ teaspoon salt

½ cup sugar

2 teaspoons lemon rind

¼ cup lemon juice

3 egg whites, stiffly beaten

Serves 4.

Dissolve gelatin in cold water. Boil water in saucepan; add salt and sugar. Remove from heat; add gelatin and stir to dissolve. Cool. Add lemon rind and juice. Refrigerate until begins to set or mounds slightly when dropped from a spoon. Beat until fluffy, then fold in beaten egg whites. Pour into glass bowl or individual serving dishes. Refrigerate. Serve with Raspberry Sauce.

RASPBERRY SAUCE

2½ cups raspberry juice

¾ cup sugar

1 tablespoon cornstarch

Dash salt

Juice of ½ lemon

Makes about 3 cups.

Pour fruit juice into saucepan. Combine sugar, cornstarch and salt; stir into juice. Cook over medium heat, stirring constantly, until thickened. Remove from heat; add lemon juice. Refrigerate; freezes well.

LEMON LIME SOUFFLÉ

Candied violets can be used for a special garnish.

10 jumbo eggs, divided

2 cups sugar, divided

½ cup lime juice

½ cup lemon juice

Zest of 2 lemons and 2 limes, grated

¼ teaspoon salt

2 tablespoons plain gelatin

½ cup light rum

Oil

3 cups whipping cream, divided

½ teaspoon vanilla

1 tablespoon sugar, or to taste

Serves 12 to 16.

Beat egg yolks until light; gradually add 1 cup sugar; beat until smooth and light in color. Add lime and lemon juices, zest and salt; stir until well blended. Place over simmering water and stir until thickened. Soak gelatin in rum; stir into custard until dissolved; cool.

Oil a 6-cup soufflé dish and wrap oiled collar around top.

Beat egg whites until stiff. Gradually fold ½ cup sugar into whites. In a chilled bowl with chilled beater, whip 2 cups cream until stiff.

Fold in remaining ½ cup sugar. Fold egg whites into custard, then fold in whipped cream. Pour into soufflé mold; chill.

Whip remaining cream; sweeten lightly; add vanilla. Garnish top of soufflé with whipped cream and twist of lime slice. Make day before for best flavor. Freezes well.

SWEDISH CREAM

Chill ahead in your best crystal sherbet dishes.

2⅓ cups heavy cream

1 cup sugar

1 envelope unflavored gelatin

1 pint sour cream

1 teaspoon vanilla

Sweetened fruit or berries

Serves 6 to 8.

Combine cream, sugar and gelatin in saucepan. Heat gently and stir until gelatin is dissolved. Cool until slightly thickened. Fold in sour cream and vanilla. Chill until firm. Top with sweetened fruit or berries.

APPLEWAY PUDDING

Smells so good while baking, like Grandma used to make; a guest said "I would buy the book just for this recipe".

1 cup raisins and chopped dates, combined

2 cups apples, peeled, cored and diced

½ cup chopped walnuts or pecans

1¼ cups flour

1 cup sugar

¼ teaspoon salt

1 teaspoon baking soda

1 teaspoon cinnamon

½ cup cold coffee

1 teaspoon vanilla

1 egg, beaten

½ cup butter (1 cube), melted

Serves 6

Place   fruit and nuts in large bowl. Sift
cor   ngredients over fruit; mix
to   ossing to coat fruit well. Add
co   a and mix well. Add egg and
butt   ...ughly. Pour into greased 8 x 8-
inch square pan. Bake at 350° for 1 hour. Serve
with lemon sauce.

LEMON SAUCE

¼ to ½ cup sugar

1 tablespoon cornstarch

1 cup water

2 to 3 tablespoons butter

½ teaspoon lemon rind, grated

1½ tablespoons lemon juice

⅛ teaspoon salt

1 drop yellow food coloring (optional)

Makes about 1 cup.

Combine sugar, cornstarch and water in the top
of a double boiler; cook over simmering water
until thickened. Remove from heat and stir in
remaining ingredients.

ENGLISH TRIFLE

"Terribly good" in the British manner.

4 egg yolks or 2 whole eggs

¼ cup sugar

1 tablespoon cornstarch

¼ teaspoon salt

1½ cups scalded milk

1 teaspoon vanilla

2 dozen ladyfingers

⅓ cup raspberry jam

½ cup (or more) sherry

1 dozen almond macaroons, crumbled

Sweetened whipped cream

Toasted blanched almonds

Maraschino or candied cherries

Serves 12.

To make soft custard, beat eggs in top of double boiler; add sugar, cornstarch and salt; gradually add scalded milk. Cook over simmering water, stirring constantly. When custard clings to metal spoon in thin coating, remove from heat. If custard should start to curdle, beat vigorously with a rotary beater until smooth. Cool quickly, covering with plastic wrap on the surface to prevent skin formation. When cool, blend in vanilla. Chill.

Split ladyfingers into halves. Stand some upright, close together, around edge of a glass bowl 8 inches in diameter and 3 inches deep. Spread remaining ladyfingers with raspberry jam and sandwich together; dip in sherry. Arrange half in bottom of bowl. Add half of cooled custard, then half of macaroon crumbs. Make layer of remaining ladyfingers; drizzle with any remaining sherry. Repeat layers of custard and crumbs. Chill at least 4 hours (may be made a day ahead). Before serving, decorate with sweetened whipped cream, almonds and cherries.

Variations: Include layers of raspberries, peaches, apricots or other fruits, in combination or individually. Reduce sherry and drizzle a good brandy over the cake layers. Substitute orange juice for sherry and brandy if no alcohol is desired.

APPLE PINWHEELS

Our testers find this a very special recipe and have made it again and again.

1¾ to 2 cups sugar

2 cups water

½ teaspoon cinnamon

½ teaspoon nutmeg

½ cup butter (1 cube)

2 cups flour

2 tablespoons sugar

2 teaspoons baking powder

1 teaspoon salt

½ cup shortening

¾ cup milk

3 tart apples, peeled and chopped or coarsely grated

Serves 6 to 8.

Combine first 4 ingredients in large saucepan; boil 5 minutes, watching to avoid boil-overs. Remove from heat; add butter in chunks; stir to melt. Set aside to cool.

Sift together flour, sugar, baking powder and salt. Cut in shortening to size of small peas. Add milk; blend just until dry ingredients are moistened uniformly. Turn out onto floured board; knead gently 3 or 4 times.

Roll into rectangle about 9 x 12 inches. Spread with apples and carefully roll up jelly-roll style. Cut into 1-inch slices; place side by side in a buttered 9 x 13-inch baking pan. Pour cooled syrup over top. Bake in a preheated 425° oven 35 to 40 minutes.

Serve warm, plain or with whipped cream or ice cream. Orange juice may be substituted for half of water; add a little grated orange rind to the syrup.

APPLE KUCHEN

May be served as a dessert or a coffee cake.

1 box yellow cake mix

½ cup butter (1 cube)

½ cup coconut

2½ cups tart apples, sliced

½ cup sugar

1 teaspoon cinnamon

1 cup sour cream

2 egg yolks, slightly beaten

Serves 8 to 10.

Cut together cake mix, butter and coconut. Press mixture into 9 x 13 x 2-inch ungreased pan. Bake 10 minutes at 350°.

Spread apples over baked crust; combine sugar and cinnamon; sprinkle over apples. Mix sour cream and egg yolks together; drizzle over top. Bake 30 to 45 minutes at 325° or until apples are tender, covering with foil first 20 to 30 minutes. Apples should be tender but not mushy, and topping golden, not brown.

Serve with unsweetened whipped cream or vanilla ice cream if desired.

BAVARIAN APPLE TORTE

A delicate apple dessert.

½ cup butter (1 cube)

⅓ cup sugar

¼ teaspoon vanilla

1 cup flour

8 ounces cream cheese, softened

¼ cup sugar

1 egg

½ teaspoon vanilla

5 cups cooking apples, peeled and thinly sliced

⅓ cup sugar

½ teaspoon cinnamon

⅓ cup sliced almonds

Serves 8 to 10.

With electric mixer, cream butter, sugar and vanilla, blend in flour. Pat dough onto bottom and 1½ inches high around sides of 9-inch springform pan.

Cream softened cheese and sugar with mixer; add egg and vanilla; beat well. Pour into pastry-lined pan.

Combine sugar and cinnamon; toss with apple slices; spoon over cream cheese layer. Sprinkle with almonds. Bake at 450° for 10 minutes; reduce heat to 400° and continue baking for 25 minutes more. Loosen torte from rim of pan but cool completely on rack before removing rim. Leave torte on bottom of pan to serve.

If desired, dust top with powdered sugar and serve with a dollop of whipped cream. Refrigerate to store.

MELBA PEAR TART

Looks elegant, tastes good, yet not too rich.

1 cup sifted flour

2 tablespoons powdered sugar

½ cup butter or margarine (1 cube), softened

3 ounces cream cheese, softened

3 tablespoons dairy sour cream

2 (16-ounce) cans pear halves, drained

½ cup raspberry preserves

1 tablespoon brandy or water

Serves 6 to 8.

Combine flour and sugar; blend in butter or margarine with fingertips. Press evenly on bottom and sides of a 9-inch flan pan or pie plate. Prick bottom with a fork. Bake 10 minutes at 450°. Cool.

Blend cream cheese and sour cream until smooth; spread in cooled crust. Arrange well-drained pears on top. Heat preserves to melt. Remove from heat; stir in brandy or water. Brush over fruit and edges of crust. Chill.

BEST-IN-THE-WEST BERRY COBBLER

A tribute to our wonderful Northwest berries.

2 to 3 cups blueberries, marionberries or blackberries

3 tablespoons shortening

1¼ cups sugar, divided

1 cup flour

1 teaspoon baking powder

¼ teaspoon salt

½ cup milk

1 tablespoon cornstarch

1 cup boiling water

Serves 4 to 6.

Spread berries in a greased 8-inch square pan. Cream shortening and ¾ cup sugar well. Sift flour, baking powder and salt together; add alternately with milk to creamed mixture. Spread batter over berries.

Combine remaining sugar and cornstarch for topping; sprinkle over batter; pour boiling water over all. Bake at 350° for 1 hour. Serve warm or at room temperature, with whipped cream or ice cream if desired.

Doubled recipe fits into a 9 x 13-inch pan.

LAKESIDE FROZEN LEMON PIE

A light, refreshing dessert after a heavy meal or in the heat of summer.

1 (9-inch) baked graham cracker crust

1 quart vanilla ice cream, softened

1 (6-ounce) can frozen lemonade concentrate, thawed

Thin lemon slices

Mint leaves

Serves 6.

Beat lemonade into softened ice cream and pour into pie shell. Freeze 4 hours or longer. Soften slightly before cutting. Garnish with lemon slices and mint.

COFFEE CREAM SUPREME

A rich coffee drink you eat with a spoon.

1½ quarts coffee ice cream

3 heaping teaspoons instant coffee

¼ cup Kahlua

¼ cup brandy

Serves 6.

Beat ice cream and instant coffee together with an electric mixer or food processor; add Kahlua and brandy. Freeze at least 3 hours. Serve in parfait glasses.

DECADENT CHOCOLATE SAUCE

A wonderful hostess gift; becomes thicker and better as it sits in the refrigerator. Try with peppermint ice cream for "double decadence".

3 cups sugar

1 cup unsweetened cocoa

2 cups sour cream

Makes 3 cups.

Combine sugar and cocoa in the top of a double boiler. With a wire whisk, beat in sour cream. Cook over simmering water, continuing to whisk, until sauce is smooth and thick, about 20 minutes. Store in refrigerator.

PIES

MELT-IN-YOUR-MOUTH PIE CRUST

A tender, crumbly crust that stays short.

2 cups sifted flour

½ teaspoon baking powder

½ teaspoon salt

¼ cup water

¾ cup Crisco

Makes 2 (8-inch) crusts.

Sift together dry ingredients. Place ⅓ cup in a small bowl; add water to make a smooth paste; set aside. Cut shortening into remaining dry ingredients until consistency is that of coarse crumbs. Add flour-water paste; toss lightly with a fork until dough forms; roll out crusts.

FIVE SHELL PIE CRUST

Easy to roll, keeps in freezer and good for pies or quiches. A crust with good flavor and color.

4 cups flour, unsifted

1 tablespoon sugar

2 teaspoons salt

1¾ cups shortening

1 tablespoon vinegar

1 large egg

½ cup water

Makes 5 crusts.

Mix first 3 ingredients, cut in shortening. In a separate bowl combine vinegar, egg and water; combine with dry ingredients. Divide dough into 5 parts; wrap each well; freeze in individual portions.

MILE HIGH LEMON PIE

A very large pie which is the essence of butter and lemon with a towering meringue; serve small portions.

1 (9 or 10-inch) baked pie shell

Filling:

1 cup plus 2 tablespoons butter (not margarine)

1½ cups sugar

3 lemons, juice and grated rind

6 egg yolks

1 whole egg

2 slices white bread, crusts removed

Meringue:

8 egg whites

1 cup plus 2 tablespoons sugar

Serves 8 to 12.

Melt butter over low heat. Stir in sugar, lemon juice and rind; heat until sugar is dissolved, stirring occasionally. Remove from heat. Beat egg yolks and whole egg together until thick. Spoon a small amount of lemon mixture into the eggs, whisking to warm eggs. Add another spoonful or two, again whisking to heat the eggs gradually. Return to saucepan and cook carefully, stirring constantly until mixture is thick and coats a spoon. Do not boil. Remove from heat.

Tear bread gently into large crumbs and scatter over bottom of baked pie crust. Spoon hot lemon mixture on top of crumbs.

Beat egg whites to a foam in large mixing bowl. Gradually add sugar, beating constantly until stiff peaks are formed. Pile over the lemon filling, sealing edges to pie shell. Brown at 350°, watching carefully so meringue does not burn, about 8 minutes, depending on oven. Cool completely. Serve at room temperature.

LEMON SOUFFLÉ PIE

Served to a Great Books discussion group and discussed in superlatives. Bake during dinner and serve while warm.

1 (9-inch) baked pie shell or 6 tart shells

1 cup sugar

5 egg yolks

Grated rind of 2 lemons

Juice of 2 lemons

2 tablespoons cornstarch

¼ cup water

Pinch salt

5 egg whites

Serves 6.

Combine egg yolks, ¾ cup sugar, lemon juice and rind, cornstarch, water and salt in top of double boiler. Cook, stirring constantly with rubber spatula until thickened. Cool slightly.

Beat egg whites until soft peaks form. Gradually add ¼ cup sugar and continue beating until stiff and glossy. Stir a small quantity of beaten egg whites into lemon mixture to lighten, then fold in remaining whites.

Pile gently into pie or tart shells. Bake in preheated 400° oven for 5 to 7 minutes; reduce heat to 300°, continue baking for 5 to 10 minutes until high and golden brown. Cool somewhat before serving. May fall a little.

UPSIDE DOWN LEMON MERINGUE PIE

The crust is a nutty meringue.

Meringue:

4 egg whites

¼ teaspoon cream of tartar

1 cup sugar

1 cup pecans or hazelnuts, finely chopped

Filling:

4 egg yolks

½ cup sugar

1 lemon, juice and grated rind

½ teaspoon unflavored gelatin

1½ cups whipping cream, whipped

Serves 8.

Beat egg whites and cream of tartar until foamy. Gradually add 1 cup sugar; beat until stiff and glossy. Fold in nuts. Line a buttered 9-inch pie pan with the meringue, making a well in center and spread to sides, building up edges. Bake at 325° for 25 minutes. Push meringue down in center and bake 25 minutes more. Cool completely.

Beat egg yolks until slightly thickened. Add juice, rind and ½ cup sugar. Cook in double boiler until it coats a spoon. Stir in gelatin; cool completely, but not until firm. Fold ⅔ of whipped cream into lemon filling. Pour into baked pie shell. Sweeten remaining whipped cream; use to garnish pie.

RHUBARB PIE

Use Melt-in-Your-Mouth Pie Crust with this pie.

1 pastry for a 2-crust (9-inch) pie

1½ cups sugar

2 tablespoons flour

2 eggs, beaten

3 cups rhubarb, cut into ¼ to ⅓-inch pieces

Serves 8.

Mix sugar and flour; add eggs, stir in rhubarb. Pour into pie shell; top with pie crust. Bake at 375° to 400° for 30 to 45 minutes.

WILD BLACKBERRY PIE WITH A DIFFERENCE

1 (9-inch) baked pie shell

1 tablespoon water

¾ teaspoon sugar

4 cups small wild blackberries

1 cup sugar

3 tablespoons cornstarch

Dash salt

2 tablespoons sugar

½ pint whipping cream, whipped

Serves 6 to 8.

Boil ¾ teaspoon sugar and water for glaze just long enough to become syrupy. Brush on baked shell to seal crust so less juice will penetrate. Wash berries and drain. Into saucepan put 2 cups of berries; mash. Combine sugar, cornstarch and salt; add to mashed berries. Cook over medium heat until thick, stirring constantly. Place remaining 2 cups of fresh berries into pie shell; sprinkle with 2 tablespoons sugar. Pour cooked berries over fresh berries in pie shell. Refrigerate until cool. Top with whipped cream. This recipe can also be used for raspberries and strawberries.

Paul Linnman

Paul Linnman

Well-known host of Portland television's "Two at Four".

PEAR CRUMBLE PIE

Great taste and eye appeal, easy to prepare. For cooking, we recommend Bosc or Bartlett pears.

1 (8-inch) unbaked pastry crust

2 cups fresh pears (6 to 7)

Lemon juice

½ cup sugar

2 tablespoons flour

⅛ teaspoon salt

1 egg, beaten

1 cup sour cream

½ teaspoon vanilla

Sprinkle of nutmeg

Crumb topping:

⅓ cup sugar

⅔ cup flour

¼ teaspoon cinnamon

¼ teaspoon nutmeg

4 tablespoons butter

Serves 6 to 8.

Peel, core and finely chop pears; sprinkle with lemon juice. Combine sugar, flour and salt in mixing bowl. Add egg, sour cream and vanilla; combine with pears. Pour into pastry shell; sprinkle with nutmeg. Bake in preheated 375° oven for 15 minutes. Reduce heat to 325°; continue to bake until firm, about 15 to 20 minutes.

Combine topping ingredients with pastry blender until crumbly. Sprinkle over pie; reheat for just a few minutes. Serve immediately.

PUMPKIN CHIFFON PIE

Even with Lake Oswego Review deadlines always hovering, star reporter Frances Davisson was known for her cooking ability; this was one of her specialties.

1 cup milk

2 cups sugar

2½ cups canned pumpkin

1 teaspoon salt

1 teaspoon ginger

1 teaspoon cinnamon

1 teaspoon nutmeg

3 eggs, separated

2 envelopes unflavored gelatin

½ cup cold water

Grated rind of 1 large orange

2 (8-inch) baked pie shells

Whipped cream

Makes 2 pies.

In double boiler, cook until thick, milk, 1 cup sugar, pumpkin, spices, and egg yolks, stirring constantly. Soak gelatin in cold water; add to thickened pumpkin mixture. Cool. Blend in remaining sugar and orange rind. Beat egg whites until stiff; fold in. Pour into pie shells and set. When firm, top with whipped cream.

Pumpkin Pecan Pie

4 slightly beaten eggs
2 cups canned or mashed cooked pumpkin
1 cup sugar
½ cup dark corn syrup
1 teaspoon vanilla

½ teaspoon cinnamon
¼ teaspoon salt
1 unbaked 9-inch pie shell
1 cup chopped pecans

Combine ingredients except pecans. Pour into pie shell—top with pecans. Bake at 350 degrees for 40 minutes, or until set.

With best wishes,   *Nancy Reagan*

SOUTHERN PECAN PIE

Truly Southern—the recipe of a Kentucky gentlewoman.

1 (9-inch) unbaked pie shell

4 tablespoons butter

¾ cup sugar

3 eggs, unbeaten

¾ cup Karo syrup

1 teaspoon lemon juice

1 cup pecans

Serves 8.

Cream butter and sugar; add eggs and beat. Add Karo and lemon juice; stir in pecans. Pour into unbaked pie shell. Bake in preheated 450° oven 10 minutes; reduce heat to 325° and continue baking for 30 to 40 minutes, until almost set in middle. (Shake pie to test degree of doneness.) Watch closely.

This pie can be made with light or dark Karo syrup. If using light syrup, use brown sugar; if using dark syrup, use granulated sugar.

FRENCH SILK AND LACE PIE

Nuts and liqueur distinguish this from other silk pies.

Shell:

2 egg whites, room temperature

¼ teaspoon cream of tartar

½ cup sugar

3 tablespoons walnuts, finely chopped

Filling:

½ cup unsalted butter (1 cube), softened

¾ cup sugar

1½ ounces unsweetened chocolate, melted and cooled

1 teaspoon vanilla

2 large eggs

1 cup whipping cream

1 tablespoon Crème de Cacao or Amaretto

½ ounce semi-sweet chocolate, shaved

Serves 8.

Beat egg whites with cream of tartar until they hold soft peaks; beat in sugar gradually until very stiff. Spread in a well buttered 9-inch pan; sprinkle bottom with nuts. Bake at 275° 1 hour; let shell cool.

Cream butter; beat in sugar ¼ cup at a time. Beat in chocolate, vanilla, then eggs, one at a time, beating well after each addition; pour into shell. Beat cream in chilled bowl until stiff; beat in liqueur. Spread cream over chocolate mixture; sprinkle with shaved chocolate. Chill at least 4 hours.

VENISON MINCEMEAT

A special gift for your hostess; beef may be substituted for venison if there's no hunter in your life.

2 to 2½ pounds venison

½ pound ground suet

5 pounds apples, peeled and chopped

2½ pounds brown sugar

3 pounds raisins

1 pound mixed glazed fruit

2 pounds currants

1 tablespoon cinnamon

2 tablespoons mace

1 tablespoon ground cloves

1 tablespoon allspice

1 tablespoon nutmeg

1 tablespoon salt

2 cups apple cider

2 cups nuts, chopped (optional)

Makes filling for 7 to 8 pies.

Boil meat until very tender. Remove meat from bones; grind or shred in a food processor. Place ground meat and all remaining ingredients except nuts in a large stockpot and cook over low heat, stirring frequently so bottom does not burn. Cook until suet is liquified and apples are tender; mixture will cook down considerably. Add nuts and cool thoroughly. Package for the freezer, about 3½ cups mincemeat for each 9-inch pie.

For each pie, line a 9-inch pie pan with pastry. Add a few tablespoons of brandy to 3½ cups mincemeat; fill crust. Top with pastry; prick well and bake in preheated 450° oven 10 minutes. Reduce heat to 350° and bake about 30 minutes longer.

CRANBERRY NUT TART

A nice addition to holiday entertaining.

Nut Crust:

3¾ cups walnuts

1 cup butter (2 cubes), softened

⅓ cup sugar

3 cups flour

1 egg, beaten

1 teaspoon vanilla

Filling:

1 envelope plain gelatin

¼ cup cold water

3 cups fresh cranberries

1 cup sugar

½ cup red currant jelly

1 cup heavy cream, whipped

Serves 10 to 12.

Finely chop nuts; mix with remaining crust ingredients; blend well. Divide mixture in half; press into two (9-inch) buttered springform pans or one (12-inch) pan. Chill for 30 minutes. Bake in preheated oven at 350° for 15 to 20 minutes, or until golden brown.

Soften gelatin in cold water. In saucepan, combine cranberries, sugar and jelly; cook for 10 minutes over low heat. Cool slightly; stir in gelatin. Cool thoroughly. Pour into crust. Chill for at least 3 hours. Serve with whipped cream.

PUTTIN' ON THE RITZ

Make this rich but light dessert a day ahead.

14 Ritz crackers, coarsely crumbled

⅔ cup nuts, chopped

3 egg whites

¾ cup sugar

½ teaspoon baking powder

Whipped cream, unsweetened

Jam

Serves 8 to 10.

Combine crumbled crackers and nuts. In a separate bowl, beat egg whites until soft peaks form. Gradually beat in sugar and baking powder until meringue is stiff and glossy. Fold in cracker-nut mixture. Spread in a well buttered 9-inch pie pan. Bake at 325° for 30 minutes. Cool; refrigerate overnight. Before serving, spread lightly with whipped cream. Serve small portions with a spoonful of a tart jam such as apricot or raspberry.

NUT TART WITH APRICOT CREAM

A superb nutty tart.

Crust:

2 cups flour

¼ cup sugar

¾ cup butter

2 egg yolks, slightly beaten

Filling:

1½ cups whipping cream

1½ cups sugar

1 teaspoon grated orange rind

2 cups walnuts, coarsely chopped

¼ teaspoon vanilla

¼ teaspoon orange extract

Serves 10 to 12.

Combine flour and sugar; cut in butter with pastry blender or food processor. Work in egg yolks with fork or continue in food processor just until dough holds together. Press evenly over ungreased bottom and sides of 11 or 12-inch tart pan with fluted sides and removable bottom. Bake at 325° for 10 minutes; color will be pale. Use hot or cold.

Combine cream, sugar, rind and salt in large saucepan. Bring to a boil, stirring constantly. Reduce heat to medium; continue cooking for 5 minutes, stirring often. Remove from heat; stir in nuts and extracts. Pour into pastry shell and bake at 375° until lightly browned, about 35 minutes for a 12-inch tart and 40 minutes for an 11-inch tart. Cool in pan on wire rack until just warm to touch. Remove sides, not bottom, and cool to room temperature. May be made a day ahead. Serve in slender wedges topped with Apricot Cream or whipped cream. May be served unadorned.

APRICOT CREAM

¼ pound dried apricots

1 cup orange juice

2 tablespoons sugar

2 tablespoons Grand Marnier

1 cup whipping cream

Makes about 3 cups.

Snip apricots into quarters. Simmer in orange juice until very soft, about 30 minutes. Remove from heat, add sugar, stir until dissolved. Cool to lukewarm; purée in blender or food processor adding Grand Marnier. Chill. Whip cream, then gently fold in apricot purée. Chill until ready to serve. Leftover Apricot Cream is delicious frozen.

CHOCOLATE CHIP SOUR CREAM CAKE

For snacks for children, bake in muffin cups 25 to 30 minutes.

1 cup butter or margarine (2 cubes)

1 cup sugar

2 eggs

2 cups flour, sifted

2 teaspoons baking powder

1 teaspoon baking soda

1 cup sour cream

1 teaspoon vanilla

Topping:

1 cup walnuts, chopped

¾ cup brown sugar

1 teaspoon cinnamon

½ cup chocolate chips

Serves 10 to 12.

Cream butter and sugar until fluffy; add eggs. Sift dry ingredients together. Blend sour cream and vanilla. Alternately add dry ingredients and sour cream to creamed mixture until all are blended.

Combine topping ingredients. Grease 10-inch tube pan. Put ⅓ topping on bottom; spoon in half the batter. Sprinkle with ⅓ topping, add remaining batter and topping. Swirl with a knife.

Bake in preheated 350° oven for 50 to 60 minutes. Cool before removing from pan. Freezes well.

CAPITOL CHOCOLATE TORTE

5 eggs

1 cup sugar

1 cup butter (2 cubes)

3 ounces semi-sweet chocolate

3 ounces unsweetened chocolate

¼ cup cornstarch, sifted

½ teaspoon vanilla

3 tablespoons orange liqueur

Glaze:

6½ ounces semi-sweet chocolate

2 tablespoons unsalted butter

⅓ cup whipping cream

Serves 16.

Over hot water in top of a double boiler, beat eggs and sugar until mixture is very light and almost white in color. Remove from heat. Meanwhile, melt the butter and skim off foam; return to heat and melt chocolate in butter. Beat the sifted cornstarch slowly into the egg mixture on low speed until thoroughly blended. Stir vanilla and orange liqueur into chocolate, then whisk chocolate mixture into egg mixture.

Spoon into a 10-inch springform which has been greased and floured. Bake at 325° for about 20 to 25 minutes until the torte pulls away from sides of pan, but a knife inserted in the center does not come out clean. Do not overbake! Cool in springform; remove ring.

To make glaze, melt chocolate and butter with cream; spoon over cool torte. Refrigerate and chill completely.

Gerry Frank

Gerry Frank

Administrative assistant to Senator Mark O. Hatfield, proprietor of Salem's Konditorei and author of "Where to: Find It, Buy It, Eat It, in New York".

PARSON'S DELIGHT

A sweet seduction.

1 package Duncan Hines Golden Butter cake mix

½ cup water

4 eggs

1 (3-ounce) package instant vanilla pudding mix

1 (4-ounce) package German's chocolate, grated

1 (6-ounce) package chocolate chips

½ cup vegetable oil

1 cup sour cream

Glaze:

1 cup powdered sugar

2 to 3 tablespoons milk

1 teaspoon vanilla

Serves 10 to 12.

Combine all ingredients in large mixing bowl; beat well. Pour into greased bundt pan. Bake at 350° for 50 to 55 minutes. Cool 20 minutes.

Combine glaze ingredients. When cake has cooled, remove from pan and glaze.

TOFFEE BOTTOM NUTMEG CAKE

Easy as a cake mix yet with an irresistable flavor and texture.

1 pound light brown sugar

3 cups flour

½ teaspoon salt

1 teaspoon baking powder

¾ cup butter or margarine, softened

½ cup pecans, finely chopped

1 egg

2 to 3 teaspoons nutmeg, freshly grated (or mace)

1½ teaspoons vanilla

1½ cups sour cream

1½ teaspoons baking soda

¾ cup pecans, coarsely chopped

Serves 12.

Preheat oven to 350°. Grease and lightly flour a 9-inch springform pan at least 2¾ inches deep with a center cone.

In large bowl combine brown sugar, flour, salt, baking powder and butter. Blend evenly with pastry blender until crumbly.

Into three cups of this mix stir ½ cup finely chopped pecans. Put this into bottom of springform pan; do not pack down.

Into remaining crumb mixture, stir egg, nutmeg and vanilla. Combine sour cream and baking soda; add to egg mixture. Add ¾ cup coarsely chopped pecans. Pour into springform.

Bake 1 hour or until cake tester comes out clean. Cool on wire rack 15 minutes; remove sides of pan. Cool completely; invert. May be served with whipped cream. Keeps well and freezes well.

NAVY BEAN BUNDT CAKE

This recipe won a prize for a young man paying his college tuition; lots of texture and distinctive flavor.

1 cup butter (2 cubes), softened

1 cup granulated sugar

⅔ cup brown sugar, firmly packed

1 tablespoon vanilla

3 eggs

1⅔ cups cooked navy beans (or canned), puréed

2 cups sifted flour

1½ teaspoons baking powder

1 teaspoon baking soda

2½ teaspoons nutmeg

2 teaspoons cinnamon

⅓ cup evaporated milk

⅓ cup water

⅓ cup chopped pecans

1⅓ cups flaked coconut

Serves 12 to 14.

In large bowl combine butter, sugars and vanilla; beat until creamy. Add eggs one at a time, beating at high speed. Stir in beans.

In medium bowl combine flour, baking powder, baking soda, nutmeg and cinnamon. Stir half dry ingredients into the creamed mixture. Stir in milk and water. Add remaining dry ingredients, stirring until blended. Add pecans and coconut. Pour into buttered and floured bundt pan.

Bake in preheated oven at 350° for 50 to 55 minutes, or until pick comes out clean. Cool thoroughly before cutting. Sift powdered sugar over cake if desired.

GRAHAM CRACKER LAYER CAKE

For best flavor, make day before serving.

1 cup margarine (2 cubes), softened

1¾ cups sugar

6 egg yolks, slightly beaten

1½ teaspoons vanilla

1⅓ cups milk

25 whole graham crackers, 2½ x 5 inches, crushed to fine crumbs

5 teaspoons baking powder

¾ cup walnuts, chopped

1 teaspoon salt

6 egg whites, beaten until soft peaks form

1½ cups whipping cream, whipped and lightly sweetened

Serves 8 to 10.

Cream together margarine and sugar. Stir in egg yolks, vanilla and milk. Add graham cracker crumbs, baking powder, walnuts and salt. Mix well. Gently fold in egg whites. Pour into 2 well-greased and floured 9-inch round cake pans. Bake at 375° for about 25 minutes. Cool in pans 5 minutes, then transfer to wire racks. When completely cool, frost with whipped cream. Chill.

MILLION DOLLAR FROSTING

This is so good that our tester almost ate the whole cake for the frosting.

¼ pound butter (1 cube), softened

¼ pound margarine (1 cube), softened

1 box powdered sugar

2 tablespoons milk

1 teaspoon vanilla

Nutmeg, freshly ground

Sprinkle of cinnamon

Enough to frost a 4 layer 8-inch cake.

Blend butter and margarine in mixer bowl. With mixer at medium speed, add powdered sugar, milk, then vanilla. Gradually build speed until on high, then beat 3 minutes or until smooth. Add fresh nutmeg and cinnamon. For chocolate frosting, add 2 envelopes unsweetened liquid baking chocolate.

COUNTY FAIR APPLESAUCE CAKE

A delicious, rich and moist spice cake complemented by coffee frosting.

2 cups flour

1 teaspoon cinnamon

1 teaspoon nutmeg

1 teaspoon cloves

Pinch salt

1 cup raisins

½ cup nuts, chopped

1 cup butter or margarine (2 cubes)

1½ cups sugar

2 eggs

2 teaspoons baking soda, dissolved in 1 tablespoon water

1½ cups applesauce

Serves 16 to 20.

Sift flour, spices and salt. Combine raisins and nuts in small bowl; add ½ cup of flour mixture; set aside. Cream butter; add sugar and beat until light. Beat in eggs. Add dry ingredients alternately with soda and applesauce. Fold raisin mixture into batter. Spoon into a greased and floured 9 x 13-inch baking pan or a tube pan. Bake at 325° for 40 to 50 minutes.

COFFEE FROSTING

2 tablespoons butter, softened

1 teaspoon vanilla

1 to 2 tablespoons strong coffee (or part cream)

2 cups confectioners' sugar, sifted

Cream cheese (optional)

Makes 1 cup.

Blend butter, vanilla and coffee. Gradually add sifted confectioners' sugar, beating well. Cream cheese may be added if desired. Frosting may be thinned with additional coffee or cream if a glaze is preferred.

MAYONNAISE CAKE

2 cups raisins

1 cup dates

2 cups nuts, chopped

2 teaspoons baking soda

1½ cups hot water

2 cups sugar

2 cups mayonnaise

2 teaspoons vanilla

2½ cups flour

2 teaspoons cinnamon

½ teaspoon salt

Serves 12.

Combine first 5 ingredients and let stand. Combine sugar, mayonnaise and vanilla; add to fruit-nut mixture. Sift together flour, cinnamon and salt; combine thoroughly with rest of ingredients. Pour into buttered 12 x 14-inch pan. Bake at 350° for 45 to 55 minutes.

APRICOT UPSIDE DOWN CAKE

The ladies of the bridge club in LeSeur, Minnesota, could never get enough of this.

4 tablespoons butter

1 cup brown sugar

1 cup or more dried apricots, cooked until tender, drained, juice reserved

3 eggs, separated

5 tablespoons apricot juice

1 cup sugar

1 cup flour

1 teaspoon baking powder

Whipped cream, sweetened

Serves 8.

Melt butter in a 9-inch cast iron skillet. Sprinkle brown sugar over butter; arrange apricots evenly, rounded side down, on butter-sugar mixture. Beat egg yolks until light; beat in apricot juice and sugar. Sift flour and baking powder together; add to egg mixture. Beat egg whites until soft peaks form; gently fold into batter. Spread over apricots.

Bake at 375° 30 to 40 minutes or until cake tests done with toothpick. As soon as cake is removed from oven, loosen it from sides of pan with a knife. Turn serving plate upside down on top of skillet, then invert skillet carefully. If necessary, rescue and rearrange any fruit or syrup that remains in skillet. Serve warm or at room temperature with a spoonful of whipped cream.

PERFECT SPONGE CAKE WITH PINEAPPLE GLAZE

1¼ cups sifted cake flour

¼ teaspoon baking powder

6 eggs

¾ teaspoon cream of tartar

1½ cups sugar

⅓ cup cold orange juice

¼ teaspoon salt

1 teaspoon vanilla

Pineapple Glaze:

2 tablespoons butter or margarine, melted

Rind of ½ small lemon, grated

1 egg yolk

3 tablespoons crushed pineapple, drained

2 tablespoons pineapple juice

1¼ cups confectioners' sugar

Serves 12.

Preheat oven to 325°. Sift flour with baking powder onto a piece of waxed paper. Separate eggs putting whites in large mixer bowl, yolks in smaller bowl. Beat whites at high speed until frothy; sprinkle in cream of tartar; continue beating until whites stand in peaks but still cling to sides of bowl. Add ½ cup sugar gradually, still beating at high speed, until meringue is smooth and satiny; set aside. Beat yolks at high speed for 2 minutes. Pour in orange juice, beating for 1 more minute at high speed. Add remaining sugar gradually; add salt and vanilla and continue beating until mixture is light and smooth.

By hand, very gently fold flour into egg yolks until batter is smooth; do not beat. Pour batter into the meringue and very gently mix well. Pour into ungreased 12-inch tube pan and bake for 1¼ hours. Cool upside down on a rack for 1 hour, then carefully ease cake away from pan with your hands. When completely cool, top with a thin coating of Pineapple Glaze.

To make glaze, beat egg yolk for 1 minute at high speed of electric mixer. Reduce speed to low and pour in melted butter, crushed pineapple, juice, lemon rind and confectioners' sugar; beat 2 minutes or until smooth. Spoon over top of sponge cake allowing some to trickle down sides.

KIRSCH CAKE

Custard Sauce:

4 egg yolks

2 cups half and half

½ cup sugar

¹⁄₁₆ teaspoon salt

3 tablespoons Kirsch

1 teaspoon vanilla

Crystallized Almonds:

3 tablespoons blanched almonds, very finely chopped

1½ tablespoons sugar

6 slices fine quality sponge cake, no more than 1 inch at thickest part

Serves 6.

In top of double boiler, thoroughly beat egg yolks, half and half, sugar and salt. Cook over hot (not boiling) water, stirring constantly, until mixture thickens slightly and coats a silver spoon. Strain. Stir occasionally until cool. Stir in Kirsch and vanilla.

Sprinkle almonds close together on a baking sheet; cover with sugar. Broil about 6 inches from heat until nuts are lightly toasted and part of sugar melts. Cool. Crumble finely.

For each serving, place one cake slice in a slightly scooped dessert plate; generously cover with custard sauce and sprinkle center with almonds.

Jane Hibler

Jane Hibler

Cookbook author and Oregonian food columnist.

GRANDMA'S BISHOP CAKE

A holiday tradition.

3 eggs

1 cup sugar

1½ cups flour, sifted

1½ teaspoons baking powder

¼ teaspoon salt

2 cups walnuts, chopped

1 cup dates, chopped

1 cup candied cherries, halved

4 ounces semi-sweet chocolate chips

Serves 15 to 20.

Combine eggs and sugar; beat until fluffy. Sift dry ingredients together into separate bowl; add nuts, fruit and chocolate; fold into egg mixture. Pour into loaf pan lined with well-buttered waxed paper.

Bake at 325° for 1½ hours; do not overbake.

BILL BAILY'S FRUIT CAKE

More fruit than cake; a holiday jewel.

1½ cups pecans, coarsely chopped

1 cup walnuts or almonds, coarsely chopped

2 cups dates, coarsely chopped

1½ cups golden raisins

1 cup red and green cherries, drained and coarsely chopped

¾ cup sifted flour

¾ cup sugar

½ teaspoon baking powder

½ teaspoon salt

3 eggs

1 teaspoon vanilla, brandy or rum

Serves 15 to 20.

Put nuts, dates, raisins and cherries in a large bowl. Sift dry ingredients over fruit-nut mixture; mix with hands until all ingredients are well coated. In a separate bowl beat eggs until frothy; add vanilla. Pour eggs over fruit-nut mixture; again mix with hands. Pour batter into greased and wax paper-lined 9½ x 5½ x 2-inch loaf pan. Bake at 300° for 1¾ hours. Cool cake. Store several days before slicing.

WHISKEY TARTS

An elegant Christmas tart.

Pastry:

1 cup butter (2 cubes)

2 (3-ounce) packages cream cheese

2 cups flour

Filling:

8 egg yolks

1¼ cups sugar

½ cup butter (1 cube)

1 cup pecans, finely chopped

1 cup coconut

1 cup candied cherries, finely chopped

1 cup raisins, chopped

⅓ cup whiskey plus a bit of rum

1 teaspoon lemon juice

Whipped cream, lightly sweetened (optional)

Nutmeg (optional)

Makes 48 small tarts.

Cream together butter and cream cheese; work in flour. Chill if soft. Roll into 48 balls and press each over bottom and sides of mini tart pans (1¾-inches). Prick bottoms with a fork. Line with foil and weight with beans or pie weights. Bake at 400° for 12 minutes. Remove lining and return to oven for 5 more minutes.

Beat egg yolks and sugar together in top of double boiler. Add butter and cook over simmering water until thick. Remove from heat and add remaining ingredients.

Put about 1 tablespoon of above mixture in baked mini tart shells; do not use too much filling. Add dab of whipped cream only slightly sweetened. Sprinkle with freshly grated nutmeg.

SWISS TARTS

Easily eaten by the dozen.

1 (8-ounce) package cream cheese, room temperature

1 cup butter (2 cubes), do not use substitute

2 cups flour

½ teaspoon salt

Jam, jelly or preserves

Powdered sugar

Makes 6 dozen.

Mix cream cheese and butter well. Add flour and salt; work together with hands. Roll very thin on well-floured board or pastry cloth. Cut into 2-inch squares. Place about ½ teaspoon jam or jelly on one half. Fold into triangle. Seal edges with fork. Place on well-greased cookie sheet.

Bake at 400° for 8 to 10 minutes or until golden brown. Shake small amount of powdered sugar over cookies while warm.

GINGERSNAPS

A great cookie for mailing; your student will love a care package with these included.

¾ cup shortening

1 cup sugar

¼ cup light molasses

1 egg, beaten

2 cups flour

2 teaspoons soda

¼ teaspoon salt

1 teaspoon cinnamon

1 teaspoon ground cloves

1 teaspoon ground ginger

Granulated sugar

Makes 4 dozen.

Cream shortening and sugar. Add molasses and egg; beat well.

Sift dry ingredients. Add to creamed mixture; mix well.

Roll dough into small walnut sized balls. Roll in sugar and place 2 inches apart on greased cookie sheet. Bake at 375° for 12 to 15 minutes.

ANESPLÄTZCHEN

Christmas is not complete without these German anise cookies. They are subtly aromatic and a nice contrast to rich buttery cookies.

3 eggs, room temperature

1 cup plus 2 tablespoons sugar

1¾ cups unsifted flour

½ teaspoon baking powder

½ teaspoon salt

1½ teaspoons anise extract

Makes 4 to 5 dozen.

Grease and flour 3 cookie sheets.

In a large mixer bowl, beat eggs at medium speed until fluffy. Gradually beat in sugar and continue beating 20 minutes more. At low speed, add dry ingredients; beat 1 minute. Add anise extract; beat just until blended.

Drop by teaspoonfuls ½ inch apart on prepared baking sheets. Swirl each to make into a circle. Let stand, uncovered, at room temperature 8 hours or overnight.

Preheat oven to 325°. Bake cookies about 10 minutes or until a creamy golden color on bottom. Do not overbake. Cool on wire racks; store in airtight containers.

THIN VANILLA COOKIES

Delicate and crisp, like Mama used to make.

½ cup butter

1 egg, beaten

⅓ cup sugar

¾ cup flour

½ teaspoon vanilla

Makes 3 dozen.

Cream butter. Add egg, sugar, flour and vanilla; mix well. Drop by teaspoonfuls on buttered cookie sheet; allow plenty of space between as they spread. With a knife dipped in cold water flatten the dough. Bake at 375° until lightly brown around edges, about 5 to 6 minutes.

NORWEGIAN BUTTER COOKIES

Sally's grandmother from Norway taught her this recipe.

1 cup butter (2 cubes)

1 cup sugar

1 egg, unbeaten

1 teaspoon almond extract

2½ cups flour, unsifted

Makes 4 to 5 dozen.

Cream butter and sugar together; add egg and flavoring; mix well. Stir in flour; chill. Using flour generously, roll thin and cut into 1 to 1½-inch rounds. Bake at 375° for 6 to 8 minutes.

Sally Struthers

Sally Struthers

Archie Bunker's daughter in "All in the Family"; Oregon-born star of movies and television.

MELTAWAYS

This attractive cookie literally melts in your mouth.

½ pound butter (2 cubes), softened

1 cup flour, unsifted

¾ cup cornstarch

⅓ cup powdered sugar

Frosting:

1 cup powdered sugar

1 teaspoon vanilla

3 ounces cream cheese

Makes about 24 cookies.

Cream ingredients together; chill dough. Roll into balls about the size of a walnut. Place one inch apart on ungreased cookie sheet. Bake at 350° about 15 minutes until barely brown. Cream together frosting ingredients. While cookies are still warm, frost. Recipe may be doubled. If not to be baked immediately, refrigerate.

ANGELLICA COOKIES

2 cups flour, sifted (more if needed)

1 cup butter (2 cubes)

4 tablespoons sugar

2 teaspoons vanilla

1 cup Oregon filberts, chopped

Powdered sugar

Makes 5 dozen.

Cream sugar and butter. Work in flour with hands, then work in nuts. Shape into balls smaller than walnuts.

Bake at 250° for 1 hour. Cookies should be solid but not browned. Roll in powdered sugar while very hot and again when cold.

Senator and Mrs. Mark O. Hatfield

He is United States Senator from Oregon; Antoinette is a celebrated cookbook author.

$1000 SUGAR COOKIES

One thousand dollars was donated to the Lakewood Center Art Gallery in exchange for this recipe.

½ cup granulated sugar

½ cup powdered sugar

½ cup margarine (1 cube)

½ cup cooking oil

1 large egg

1 teaspoon vanilla

½ teaspoon almond extract

2½ cups flour

½ teaspoon soda

½ teaspoon cream of tartar

¼ teaspoon salt or less

Makes 6 dozen.

Combine sugars, margarine, oil, egg and flavorings in electric mixer. Sift dry ingredients; add and mix well. Drop dough on cookie sheets in small mounds, between a filbert and a walnut in size, 24 to a sheet. Press centers firmly with small glass dipped in granulated sugar. Bake at 375° for 8 minutes or until just beginning to show color. Cool. Handle and store carefully.

CRISS CROSS COOKIES

½ cup shortening

¾ cup sugar

1 egg

½ teaspoon lemon extract

1¾ cups flour

¾ teaspoon cream of tartar

¾ teaspoon soda

¼ teaspoon salt

1 cup white seedless raisins

Makes 3 dozen cookies.

Cream shortening and sugar until fluffy; add egg and beat well. Add lemon extract. Stir in dry ingredients and raisins.

Roll dough into balls the size of large walnuts. Place 3 inches apart on lightly greased baking sheet. Flatten each ball with fork in a criss cross pattern. Bake at 375° for 8 to 10 minutes.

Kay Griffin Vega

Kay Vega

Lake Oswego Community Theater executive producer and tap dancer par excellence.

BULL MOUNTAIN RAISIN SUGAR COOKIES

Submitted by Elsie Ames, well known in the Portland area for her gift shop and philanthropies.

1½ cups raisins

1½ cups water

1 cup shortening

1½ cups sugar

2 eggs

3½ cups flour

½ teaspoon salt

1 teaspoon baking powder

1 teaspoon baking soda

1 teaspoon vanilla

Granulated sugar

Makes 5 dozen.

Combine raisins and water in small saucepan; cook until all water is absorbed. Cool.

Cream shortening and sugar until light and fluffy. Add eggs and beat well. Add sifted dry ingredients, vanilla and raisins; mix together. Form into small balls and roll in sugar. Place on lightly greased cookie sheet; press with a flat-bottomed glass. Bake at 350° for 10 minutes.

SESAME CRISPS

A national baking contest prize winner.

2 cups butter (1 pound), softened

1½ cups sugar

3 cups flour

1 cup sesame seeds

2 cups coconut, finely shredded

½ cup almonds, finely chopped

Makes 4 to 5 dozen.

Cream butter; gradually add sugar and beat until light and fluffy. Add flour; mix thoroughly. Stir in sesame seeds, coconut and almonds. Divide dough in thirds. On sheets of waxed paper, form each into a long roll about 1¼ to 2 inches in diameter. Wrap snugly and refrigerate until firm.

With a sharp, thin knife, cut slices ⅛ to ¼-inch thick. Bake on ungreased cookie sheets at 300° 20 to 30 minutes, depending on size. Cool on wire racks.

TENNIS BALLS

Travels well in a back pack and in brown bag lunches; sent to us by a tennis professional and coach.

2 cups butter (1 pound)

1 cup sugar

1 teaspoon vanilla

3½ cups flour

2 cups potato chips, crushed (1 twin-pack bag)

½ cup pecans, chopped

Makes 7 dozen.

Cream butter, sugar and vanilla; stir in flour. Add potato chips and nuts. Drop teaspoonfuls of dough onto greased cookie sheet; they do not spread. Bake at 350° for 15 minutes.

NEARLY PERFECT COOKIES

The flavor of orange is a surprise. Cookies keep beautifully and the recipe makes a large batch.

3½ cups flour

1 teaspoon baking soda

1 teaspoon salt

1 cup rolled oats

½ cup flaked coconut

½ to 1 cup chopped nuts

1 cup crushed cornflakes

1 (8-ounce) package chocolate chips

1 cup butter or margarine (2 cubes)

1 cup brown sugar, firmly packed

1 cup granulated sugar

2 eggs

1 cup salad oil

1 teaspoon vanilla

Grated rind of one orange

Makes 8 dozen.

Sift together flour, soda and salt; set aside. Combine oats, coconut, nuts, crushed cereal and chocolate chips; set aside.

In large mixer bowl, cream butter. Beat in sugars; cream until fluffy. Add eggs and beat well. Add oil, vanilla and orange rind; mix well. Add sifted dry ingredients; beat to combine. Add remaining ingredients.

Place mounds the size of small walnuts on ungreased cookie sheets. Flatten with a fork dipped in flour. Bake in preheated 325° oven for 10 to 15 minutes.

AMAZIN' HAZEN COOKIES

Ben Franklin would have loved these; deposits in your cookie jar won't stay long enough to earn interest.

1 cup shortening

1 cup granulated sugar

1 cup brown sugar

2 eggs

¼ cup Wesson oil

1 teaspoon vanilla

1 cup flour, unsifted

1 teaspoon baking powder

1 teaspoon cinnamon

½ teaspoon salt

1 cup walnuts, chopped

1 cup raisins or chocolate chips

1½ cups oatmeal

Makes 6 to 8 dozen.

Cream shortening and sugars together. Add eggs, oil and vanilla; mix well.

Combine dry ingredients with the creamed mixture. Add raisins, nuts, and oatmeal. Mix well.

Grease pan lightly or spray with non-stick coating. Drop by teaspoonfuls onto cookie sheet; press down if you desire a thin, crisp cookie. These spread, so leave room, 20 cookies to a sheet. Bake at 350° for 10 minutes. Remove from cookie sheet as soon as possible. Cool in brown paper bags; store in covered container.

CHOCOLATE MERINGUE PUFFS

Fragile and delicious.

1 (6-ounce) package semi-sweet chocolate chips

2 egg whites

Dash salt

¾ cup powdered sugar

½ teaspoon white vinegar

½ teaspoon vanilla

½ cup walnuts, chopped

Makes 3½ dozen.

Melt chocolate over low heat. Beat egg whites with salt until foamy. Gradually add sugar, beating continuously until stiff and glossy. Beat in vinegar and vanilla. Very gently fold in melted chocolate and nuts.

Drop by teaspoonfuls onto ungreased cookie sheet. Bake at 350° for 10 minutes. Cool on rack.

HELLO DOLLY COOKIES

½ cup margarine (1 cube)

1 cup graham cracker crumbs

1 cup coconut

1 package chocolate chips

1 cup nuts

1 can Eagle Brand condensed milk

Makes 3 dozen squares.

Melt margarine in a 9 x 12-inch pan. Pour cracker crumbs, coconut, chocolate chips and nuts into pan one layer at a time, spreading each evenly. Pour Eagle Brand over all. Bake 30 minutes at 350°. Let cool completely before cutting.

Carol Channing

Carol Channing

Everybody's favorite Dolly Levi, vibrant star of stage and screen.

ALMOND SQUARES

Incredibly delicious, watch them disappear.

2 cups graham cracker crumbs

2 tablespoons brown sugar

½ cup butter (1 cube), melted

1 can sweetened condensed milk

1 (7-ounce) package coconut

1 teaspoon vanilla

Topping:

1 (6-ounce) package chocolate chips

1 (6-ounce) package butterscotch chips

4 tablespoons butter

6 tablespoons chunky peanut butter

⅓ cup almonds, chopped

Makes 3 dozen squares.

Mix first 3 ingredients. Pat into a greased 9 x 13-inch pan. Bake at 325° for 10 minutes. Cool.

Combine next three ingredients; pour over baked crust. Bake at 325° for 25 minutes. Cool.

Melt topping ingredients in top of double boiler. Spread over top. Cool and cut into squares.

PECAN TURTLE BARS

A surprisingly easy cookie that mails well.

2 cups flour

1 cup brown sugar, packed

½ cup butter (1 cube)

1 cup pecan halves

Caramel Layer:

½ cup brown sugar, packed

⅔ cup butter

Topping:

12 ounces semi-sweet chocolate chips

Makes 50 squares.

At medium speed, combine flour, brown sugar and butter to make fine particles. Pat into ungreased 9 x 13-inch baking pan. Sprinkle pecans on top.

Combine brown sugar and butter in saucepan; cook over medium heat, stirring constantly; boil 1 minute. Pour over pecans and crust. Bake at 350° for 18 minutes. Caramel layer should be bubbly. Remove from oven. Sprinkle chocolate chips over top; spread evenly as they melt. Cool and cut into squares.

SINFULLY DELICIOUS CARAMEL SQUARES

These are wonderfully immoral—a confection more than a cookie.

1 cup butter (2 cubes)

1 cup flour

½ teaspoon salt

½ teaspoon baking soda

1 cup brown sugar

1½ cups quick rolled oats

48 light caramels

6 tablespoons cream

4 tablespoons flour

1 cup chocolate chips

1 cup nuts, chopped (optional)

Makes 3 dozen.

Cut butter into dry ingredients until crumb mixture forms. Set aside 1 cup; press remaining crumbs into a greased 9 x 13-inch pan. Bake at 350° for 10 minutes.

Melt caramels and cream in top of double boiler. Blend in flour. Spread over cookie base.

Sprinkle chocolate chips and nuts over caramel mixture. Top with reserved crumb mixture. Bake at 350° for 12 to 15 minutes. Cut into squares.

ALMOND ROCA BARS

1 cup butter (2 cubes), do not use substitute

½ cup brown sugar

½ cup granulated sugar

1 egg yolk

1 cup flour

1 teaspoon baking powder

6 (1.45-ounce) Hershey bars

1 to 1½ cups almonds, finely chopped

Makes 3 dozen.

Cream together butter and sugars. Add egg yolk and blend. Combine flour and baking powder; add to above. Spread evenly in a 9 x 13-inch pan. Bake at 325° for 25 minutes.

Remove from oven and immediately arrange Hershey bars on top. Spread evenly as chocolate softens, then sprinkle with chopped nuts. Cut while warm. Refrigerate to set, but serve at room temperature.

FROSTED BROWNIES

A chocoholic's dream.

4 (1-ounce) squares unsweetened chocolate

1 cup butter (2 cubes)

2 cups sugar

3 eggs, beaten

1 teaspoon vanilla

1 cup walnuts, coarsely broken

1 cup flour, sifted

¼ teaspoon salt

Frosting:

1 (6-ounce) package semi-sweet chocolate chips

2 to 3 tablespoons butter

3 tablespoons milk

1 cup powdered sugar, sifted

Makes 2 dozen.

Melt chocolate and butter in a double boiler. Remove from heat and add sugar, eggs and vanilla; mix well. Add walnuts. Sift flour and salt together; add gradually and mix well. Pour into greased 9 x 9-inch pan lined with waxed paper. Bake at 350° for 45 to 50 minutes. Cool completely before frosting.

Combine chips, butter and milk in saucepan. Stir over low heat until chocolate is just melted. Remove from heat and stir in sugar; beat until glossy. Cover brownies thickly.

TEXAS PRALINES

These are so good that they inspired our testers to make an Oregon variety.

1 cup granulated sugar

2 cups brown sugar, packed

3 tablespoons butter

1 cup half and half

¼ teaspoon salt

2 cups pecans or walnuts

¼ teaspoon cinnamon

1 teaspoon maple flavoring

Makes 3 to 5 dozen.

Combine sugars, butter, cream and salt. Blend and stir over medium heat until boiling; cover for three minutes so that steam washes sugar crystals from sides. Bring slowly to 238° on candy thermometer (soft ball stage), stirring. Remove from heat, cool 5 minutes, add nuts and flavorings. Beat until creamy and just beginning to thicken. Immediately drop by tablespoonfuls (teaspoonfuls for smaller pralines) onto marble slab or waxed paper; let cool and harden. When cold, wrap each separately with foil or clinging wrap. Store in covered tin but best served fresh.

OREGON PRALINES: Substitute toasted hazelnuts for pecans. Omit cinnamon and substitute vanilla for maple extract.

CHOCOLATE CRUNCH TOFFEE

Tastes like a Heath bar.

40 soda crackers

1 cup butter (2 cubes)

1 cup brown sugar

1 (12-ounce) package chocolate chips

1 cup nuts, chopped (optional)

Makes 80 squares.

Preheat oven to 350°. Line jelly roll pan with foil and spray with vegetable oil. Place soda crackers in pan in single layer.

Combine butter and brown sugar in saucepan and bring to a boil. Boil 3 minutes, then pour over crackers and spread evenly. Bake for 5 minutes (crackers will float). Remove from oven and sprinkle with chocolate chips, spreading evenly as they melt; if necessary, return toffee to oven long enough to melt chips. Sprinkle with nuts if desired. Cut into squares while warm.

TRINITY ROCA

So delicious and so easy — the favorite of an annual holiday bazaar.

2 cups butter (1 pound)

2 cups sugar

1 cup almonds, blanched and toasted

1 (12-ounce) package semi-sweet chocolate
   chips

1 cup ground walnuts or pecans

Makes about 3 pounds.

Melt butter; add sugar and almonds; cook until bubbling hot and golden brown. Spread in large metal pan. Sprinkle chocolate chips on top, spreading evenly as they melt. Top with ground nuts. Cover with foil and refrigerate at least 4 hours. Leaving foil in place, invert pan and hit bottom to release candy. Break into pieces. Store in tightly covered tin.

PEANUT BUSTER BARS

Quick to make and a children's favorite.

1 (12-ounce) package chocolate chips

1 (12-ounce) package butterscotch chips

1 cup peanut butter

12 ounces unsalted peanuts

1 (10½-ounce) bag miniature marshmallows

Makes 24 squares.

Melt chips in top of double boiler; add peanut butter and stir to blend. Combine nuts and marshmallows in large mixing bowl; add chocolate mixture and toss to coat evenly. Press into lightly buttered 9 x 13-inch pan. Chill well; cut into squares.

SWEDISH NUTS

A nice gift from your kitchen

1½ cups blanched almonds

2 cups walnut halves

2 egg whites

Dash salt

1 cup sugar

½ cup butter (1 cube)

Makes 8 cups.

In a broiler pan or other large, shallow baking pan, roast nuts at 325° until light brown. Add salt to egg whites; beat until soft peaks form. Gradually add sugar and continue beating until very stiff and glossy. Fold in nuts.

Melt butter in the large baking pan. Add nut mixture and bake at 275° for 35 minutes, stirring every 10 minutes; use all the butter (it will be absorbed with stirring). Watch carefully to avoid burning. Cool and store in tightly covered tins.

GRANOLA

Makes a great "care" package.

4 cups rolled wheat

4 cups rolled oats

2 cups wheat germ

1 cup bran

2 cups sunflower seeds

2 cups coconut

2 cups soy flakes

2 cups rolled rye

2 cups sesame seeds

1½ cups honey

2 tablespoons vanilla

2 cups cooking oil

1 cup almonds

1 cup dried fruit (apple nuggets, raisins, apricots, etc.)

Makes 24 cups.

Combine dry ingredients in a large container. Heat honey, vanilla and oil; pour over cereals and toss to coat evenly. Spread ½ to ¾ inch thick in shallow baking pans. Bake at 200° to 225° for 1 hour, stirring mixture every 15 minutes. Empty while hot into a large brown bag to cool. When cool, add almonds and fruit. Place in plastic bags; freeze to maintain freshness.

Other grains such as rolled barley may be substituted, but proportions should be the same.

Epilogue

CONTRIBUTORS

Marcia Abelson
Lola Abrahams
Phyllis Akin
Elsie Ames
Barbara Anderson
Robert and Sally Bailey
Bill and Donna Baily
Helen Baker
Sonia Baker
Sandy Baldwin
Frances Baunach
Betty Bennett
Sali Bernhardt
Anne Black
Ailsa Bloodworth
Carol Bond
Joanne Bonime
Margie Boulé
Mae C. Bradshaw
Mary Branda
Clary Brickner
Jenneva Briggs
Marjorie Briggs
Betty Brooks
Sally Brustad
Carol Brusie
Roger and Mary Beth Burpee
Sally Burpee
Julia Butler
Charles and Susan Cameron
Peggy Campbell
Virginia Campbell
Joyce Carlos
Becky Carrier
Marlis Carson
Trudy Carter
Carol Channing
Carol Clay
Eileen Colhouer
Betty Cook

Jane Coombs
Priscilla Coombs
Marge Cortese
Mrs. Herbert E. Conner
M. Cunningham
Christine Davis
Lora Davis
Maureen Davis
Maxyne Davis
Frances Davisson
Carol Dean
Ann Deering
Dorothy A. Deich
Mary Deich
Dee Denton
Kay DeGreef
Wendy DeHart
Margaret deLuccia
Stephanie Detjens
James & Ginette DePreist
V'Anne Didzun
Dorothy Drinker
Ann Durfee
Barbara Dutton
Alyce Dell Dutton
Fae Eick
Genda Edwards
Eloise Evans
Jonelle Fairchild
Ruth Forrester
Margaret Fowler
Virginia Fowlks
Gerry Frank
Yvonne Fraunfelder
Melanie Galdarisi
Mrs. Elburt Gardner
Marilyn Gatto
Beth Gerber
DeDe Gillespie
Kay Glazer

Barbara Goecks
Lori Goldadi
Jean Graham
John Graham
Barilynn Grant
Jean Green
Florence L. Gulmary
Wayne and Lynn Hamersly
Barbara Hamlin
Carol Halvorson
Leah Hardin
Irene Harrison
Ed Hash
Senator and Mrs.
    Mark O. Hatfield
Robert H. Hazen
Helen Heestand
Jan Henrotin
Jane Hibler
Susan Hobson
Millie Hoelscher
Helga Hoffmann
Bob Hope
Louise Houston
Karen Howells
Jana Huffhines
Mrs. Fred Hughes
Ceil Huntington
E. Inman
Emma Lou Johnson
Dorothy Fisher Jones
Mickey Jones
Michele Joseph
Elaine Kallas
Arlene Kampe
Marie Kaseberg
Karen Kemp
Beth Kennedy
Charlotte Kern
Judy Kershaw

Gorel Kinersly
Betty Kingsbury
Anita Koch
Gwen Kuhn
Maxine R. Larsen
Sue Lauritzen
Nancy Leatherman
Linda Lee
Norman and Alice Leyden
Kathy Lindeman
Linda Lindsey
Paul Linnman
Millie Little
Lin Loen
June Lofgren
Maureen Long
Marla Love
Kay Lund
Maybelle C. MacDonald
Horst Mager
Linda Manning
Kathy Martin
Johnny Mathis
Wana Maurer
Anita McCloskey
Judy McCuddy
Harriet McEvers
Anne McGranahan
Maude McKinley
Linda McKnight
Renate Merrill
Annie Miller
Laura Mold
Naome Morgan
Marguerite Morin
Janet Moore
Lois Mowry
Virginia Mullen
A. Murphy
Anne Myers
Paul Newman
Kathy Niemi

Ann North
Vana O'Brien
Marian O'Connor
Reba Owen
Bob and Marilyn Pamplin
Pat Parker
Fern Parrish
Dorothy M. Patrick
Ann Phillips
Julianne Phillips
Kelley Phillips
Pam Pianalto
Mrs. John Praegner
Jean Radow
Sandy Ragen
John Raitt
Julie Rea
President and Mrs.
    Ronald Reagan
Kay Rhoney
Donna Roberge
Cliff Robertson
Alyce Rogers
Caroline Rogg
Dorothy Romberg
Sue Rommel
Linda Ronchelli
Elizabeth Ross
Richard Ross
Pete Rossini
Melba Roth
Dorie Russell
Nancy H. Sampson
Donna Scales
Dolores Schmidt
Irene E. Schultz
Nancy Sergeant
Billy Jean Siler
Beverly Sills
Reone Smith
Nancy Spitznass
Sally Stark

Elaine Stevens
Sally Stevens
Elizabeth Stockman
Carol Strader
Sally Struthers
Thelma Sweeney
Mary Ann Swinford
Hortense Sylvester
Jean Snyder
Karen Taylor
Phyllis Thaxter
June Tofte
Anna Thomas
Carol Thomas
Valorie Thomas
Joyce Thornton
Gerri Tisdel
Hazel Todd
Nancy Todd
Norma Todd
Adrienne Tromley
Relna Tromley
Mrs. John Trullinger
Marianne VanWitzenburg
Kay Vega
Veronica Vybiral
Lindsay Wagner
Barbara Weirich
Marilyn Williams
Mrs. Walter R. Williams
Jackie Willis
Janet Wizer
Linda Woods
Sheila Woolworth
Grace Wygal
Rachel Young
Marilyn Zeigler

INDEX

Crustless Crab Quiche 140
Sausage Soufflé 138
Easter Eggs Casserole 137
Savery Eggs Casserole 136
Fancy Egg Scramble 135
Deep Dish Lasagne 85
* Marzetti 83
* Calif Casserole 82
Veal Medallions 74
Scandinavian Soup 56
(dessert)

Salad - confetti cabbage 182
green pasta w/... 186

Potato Clouds 160
* Puttin' On The Ritz (pie) 213
Sour Crm Enchiladas 113
Chicken Hash 110

Rave Revues
LAKEWOOD CENTER
P.O. Box 274 • Lake Oswego, OR 97034

Please send _____ copies of *Rave Revues* at $18.95 plus $3.00 postage and handling to: (Add $1.00 per book for gift wrapping)

Name _____

Address _____

City/State _____ Zip _____

Make checks payable to *Rave Revues* Lakewood Center

Visa/MasterCard # _____ exp. date _____ Signature _____

From: *Rave Revues*
LAKEWOOD CENTER
P.O. Box 274 • Lake Oswego, OR 97034

To:
Name _____
Address _____
City _____
State _____ Zip _____
MAILING LABEL—PLEASE PRINT

Rave Revues
LAKEWOOD CENTER
P.O. Box 274 • Lake Oswego, OR 97034

Please send _____ copies of *Rave Revues* at $18.95 plus $3.00 postage and handling to: (Add $1.00 per book for gift wrapping)

Name _____

Address _____

City/State _____ Zip _____

Make checks payable to *Rave Revues* Lakewood Center

Visa/MasterCard # _____ exp. date _____ Signature _____

From: *Rave Revues*
LAKEWOOD CENTER
P.O. Box 274 • Lake Oswego, OR 97034

To:
Name _____
Address _____
City _____
State _____ Zip _____
MAILING LABEL—PLEASE PRINT

Rave Revues
LAKEWOOD CENTER
P.O. Box 274 • Lake Oswego, OR 97034

Please send _____ copies of *Rave Revues* at $18.95 plus $3.00 postage and handling to: (Add $1.00 per book for gift wrapping)

Name _____

Address _____

City/State _____ Zip _____

Make checks payable to *Rave Revues* Lakewood Center

Visa/MasterCard # _____ exp. date _____ Signature _____

From: *Rave Revues*
LAKEWOOD CENTER
P.O. Box 274 • Lake Oswego, OR 97034

To:
Name _____
Address _____
City _____
State _____ Zip _____
MAILING LABEL—PLEASE PRINT

Rave Revues
LAKEWOOD CENTER
P.O. Box 274 • Lake Oswego, OR 97034

Please send _____ copies of *Rave Revues* at $18.95 plus $3.00
postage and handling to: (Add $1.00 per book for gift wrapping)

Name _____

Address _____

City/State _____ Zip _____

Make checks payable to *Rave Revues* Lakewood Center

Visa/MasterCard # _____ exp. date _____ Signature _____

From: **Rave Revues**
LAKEWOOD CENTER
P.O. Box 274 • Lake Oswego, OR 97034

To: Name _____

Address _____

City _____

State _____ Zip _____

MAILING LABEL—PLEASE PRINT

Rave Revues
LAKEWOOD CENTER
P.O. Box 274 • Lake Oswego, OR 97034

Please send _____ copies of *Rave Revues* at $18.95 plus $3.00
postage and handling to: (Add $1.00 per book for gift wrapping)

Name _____

Address _____

City/State _____ Zip _____

Make checks payable to *Rave Revues* Lakewood Center

Visa/MasterCard # _____ exp. date _____ Signature _____

From: **Rave Revues**
LAKEWOOD CENTER
P.O. Box 274 • Lake Oswego, OR 97034

To: Name _____

Address _____

City _____

State _____ Zip _____

MAILING LABEL—PLEASE PRINT

Rave Revues
LAKEWOOD CENTER
P.O. Box 274 • Lake Oswego, OR 97034

Please send _____ copies of *Rave Revues* at $18.95 plus $3.00
postage and handling to: (Add $1.00 per book for gift wrapping)

Name _____

Address _____

City/State _____ Zip _____

Make checks payable to *Rave Revues* Lakewood Center

Visa/MasterCard # _____ exp. date _____ Signature _____

From: **Rave Revues**
LAKEWOOD CENTER
P.O. Box 274 • Lake Oswego, OR 97034

To: Name _____

Address _____

City _____

State _____ Zip _____

MAILING LABEL—PLEASE PRINT

mini Quiche Lorraines 17